# Gould Library

## Paoli Presbyterian Church

Paoli,
Pennsylvania

Dedicated 1998

# DISCIPLINES of GRACE

## fROM SPIRITUAL ROUTINES to SPIRITUAL RENEWAL

## t.m.mOORE

InterVarsity Press
Downers Grove, Illinois

*InterVarsity Press*
*P.O. Box 1400, Downers Grove, IL 60515-1426*
*World Wide Web: www.ivpress.com*
*E-mail: mail@ivpress.com*

*InterVarsity Press® is the book-publishing division of InterVarsity Christian Fellowship/USA®, a student movement active on campus at hundreds of universities, colleges and schools of nursing in the United States of America, and a member movement of the International Fellowship of Evangelical Students. For information about local and regional activities, write Public Relations Dept., InterVarsity Christian Fellowship/USA, 6400 Schroeder Rd., P.O. Box 7895, Madison, WI 53707-7895.*

*All Scripture quotations, unless otherwise indicated, are taken from the* King James Version.

*The poem "I Heard the Sound of Armies Marching" first appeared in* The Formalist *2, no. 2 (2000).*

*The poem "Borrowed Words" by Steven Wright is used by permission of the author.*

*Cover photograph: Roderick Chen / SuperStock*

*ISBN 0-8308-2299-2*

*Printed in the United States of America* ∞

Library of Congress Cataloging-in-Publication Data

*Moore, T. M. (Terry Michael), 1949-*
*Disciplines of grace : from spiritual routine to spiritual renewal / T. M. Moore.*
*p. cm.*
*Includes bibliographical references.*
*ISBN 0-8308-2299-2 (pbk. : alk. paper)*
*1. Spiritual life—Christianity. I. Title.*
*BV4501.2 .M5827 2001*
*248.4—dc21*

*2001024414*

*26  25  24  23  22  21  20  19  18  17  16  15  14  13  12  11  10  9  8  7  6  5  4  3  2  1*

*23  22  21  20  19  18  17  16  15  14  13  12  11  10  09  08  07  06  05  04  03  02  01*

*For Lane and Annette Adams*

# contents

# Introduction

We've all known them—those seasons when the wind seems to go out of the sails of our spiritual lives. Our time in the Word of God is unexciting and unfruitful. Prayer is a struggle. Worship never quite satisfies. Our devotions are skimpy or even skipped. Our witness is virtually nonexistent. Too many things seem more important than spirituality, and we would not describe ourselves as "currently on the cutting edge of Christian growth."

Yet we love the Lord and truly want to serve him, we are faithful in our church life and worship, and we feel hopeful and assured as to our eternal home. We're hungry for him but aren't finding the satisfaction we seek. Somehow things just aren't clicking, not spiritually anyway.

There are undoubtedly many reasons why we find ourselves in the spiritual doldrums from time to time, why the sails of our spirits go limp while the rest of our life is proceeding full speed ahead. But this is not a book of diagnoses. Nobody needs to tell us when we're spiritually becalmed, and a lot of navel gazing about why or how we got in this situation would not be particularly helpful. What we want is out, or rather, back on course with the Lord, our spiritual sails filled with the powerful winds of his Spirit once again. We want our devotions to come alive, our worship to flare anew with spiritual fire, the bounce to return to our spiritual step. We want to rediscover the presence of the Lord, to experience his glory and to bask afresh in the certainty and warmth of his mercy and grace. We yearn for the Word to speak clearly and powerfully to us. We long to know the assurance that our prayers are being heard and to experience the filling of God's Spirit in fresh, new gusts of power and life. We want our hearts to pound with love for our God, and we want to be able to show that love more fervently and consistently to the people around us.

However we may have arrived at the spiritual doldrums, this much is certain: within the disciplines of grace—Scripture reading, prayer, worship, special time devoted to the Lord and all the rest—lies the key to our recovery. For the Spirit of God is still blowing in those arenas as faithfully and powerfully as ever. The problem is that our sails have become tattered and in need of repair, and frankly, some of them have never been unfurled to catch his life-giving wind.

It may well be that at such times of spiritual stasis our spiritual disciplines are in disrepair. They have become mere routines—mindless, joyless, fruitless activities—and are no longer serving the purpose of helping us grow in the grace of the Lord. We know these exercises are important, and so we press on in them as we always have to the best of our ability. But something is missing. We feel like we're just going through the motions, without a sense of the Spirit or glory of God in our times of devotion. Something needs to happen to help us break out of the doldrums of spiritual routine in which we are languishing so that we can catch the powerful winds of God's Spirit in the practice of spiritual disciplines and be genuinely renewed.

In the chapters that follow I share some of what others and I have learned over the years about the disciplines of grace, those special tools and means that God has provided to help us grow in him. My purpose, besides giving praise and thanks to the God of unceasing mercy and grace, is that of one frequently forlorn sailor who would like to lend a hand to another. The chapters that follow offer many suggestions for moving from routine to renewal in the practice of spiritual disciplines. Not all of them will appeal to or work for you. However, some of them should, as the Lord leads you to chart a course of renewal under the guidance of his Spirit.

The winds of God's Spirit are still blowing, and his power is ready to help you get moving once again. You can sense it because you have been there before and known the power of God's Spirit carrying you along on the river of grace. Often he has touched your heart with something from his Word and profoundly changed your life as a result. He has acknowledged and answered your prayers and filled you with the joy of assurance. He has given you strength to resist temptation and power to be his witness. He has helped you grow in love for him and for others in surprising, wonderful ways. All this he has certainly done at times. But such times of spiritual exhilaration and advance do not have to be the exception. We have every reason to expect them to be more and more the norm.

This is a practical book—more a handbook for personal spiritual renewal than a theology of spiritual disciplines. It invites you to enter anew into the disciplines of grace, to discover some keys to a consistently vibrant devotional life of growth in the grace and knowledge of the Lord. Read each chapter carefully—hopefully with another person or a group. Use the discussion questions to guide you into self-examination, seeking the Lord and charting a course for renewal. Take your time. My prayer is that you will be encouraged that your practice of the disciplines of grace can be a time for meeting the Lord Jesus face to face with greater consistency and power, to behold his glory, know his presence and fill up with love for him and your neighbor.

My purpose is to help you discover some ways of breaking out of the doldrums of routine and recovering the practice of the disciplines of grace as God intends. I am grateful to Andy Le Peau, the staff at Inter-Varsity Press, those who read earlier drafts of this manuscript and made many helpful suggestions, and especially my wife, Susie, for their encouragement and assistance in this project.

The way to renewal may not be easy at times; great strides in anything never are. But the blessing to be found in recovering the grace and power available in the practice of spiritual disciplines is worth any sacrifice, any struggle. And it's waiting just ahead for you.

# 1

# DISCIPLINES OR ROUTINES?

*Modern Christians are not lacking in "relevance." What they do lack is
a disciplined life and a critical mind to resist the temptation to conform to
what everybody thinks or does.*
SIMON CHAN

*But grow in grace, and in the knowledge of our Lord and Saviour Jesus Christ.*
2 PETER 3:18

*I* played football in college. Well, I should qualify that: I was on
the football team—I never really played much. At the end of each school
year every team member would adopt a series of personal disciplines that
he was expected to follow over the summer. The idea was, by the time we
returned in the fall, we would be in good shape and hopefully a little
stronger and faster and more adept at our individual positions than when
we left school in May. Typically, those disciplines would include weight
training, running, dietary controls and honing of techniques, and the
coaching staff expected us to devote serious time and energy to those disciplines every day. Each week we were supposed to increase how far we
could run in twelve minutes, the amount of weight we could lift in different exercises, excess body weight lost or "relocated," and our skills at
such techniques as blocking, quickness, lateral movement and so forth.

Many of my fellow teammates devoted themselves to those disciplines, making them the centerpiece of their summer. They worked hard,
sacrificed much and immersed themselves fully in their personal plans

and disciplines. They loved to work out and, each fall, were stronger and faster than when they had left school in May. They were the ones who played. For my part, I never gave more than half-hearted attention to any of the disciplines that I would go away from school in good faith determined to engage in daily. My intentions were noble, but somehow it was too much trouble. I never pushed myself—in running, exercising or lifting weights. That is, when I managed to do them at all. I did just enough work on my techniques to keep from falling back in the depth chart (I was number two at my position but definitely not trying harder). It just seemed like my mind was always somewhere else, thinking about this or that and keeping me from focusing my attention on the business at hand. I barely tolerated the time I invested in these activities and cut it short more often than not. I skipped or skimped on my daily disciplines as often as I carried them out. I did just enough of each discipline to be able to say to my coaches that I had kept up my routine pretty well throughout the summer. But I never got much stronger or faster, and I never improved sufficiently in the skills required by my position to log many minutes of play. I sincerely hoped at the end of each school year that my summer would be sufficiently disciplined to enable me to get a little more playing time in the fall. But this usually turned out to be three months of half-hearted routines, with little in the way of improvement to show for my trouble.

There are some fundamental differences between routines and disciplines. While each is essential to life, they are not the same. For this reason, maintaining disciplines and not allowing them to lapse into mere routines is very important. And nowhere is this as important as in our spiritual lives, where, for too many followers of Christ, the disciplines of grace that God has given us to help us grow in him have become routine activities devoid of life-changing power.

### Routines and Disciplines

A routine is something we do in order to maintain a status quo, like brushing our teeth and getting ready for the day, changing the oil in our car, locking the doors and turning out the lights before we retire each evening, or making the bed each morning. Such routines have an important place in our lives, but they do not change or improve anything. They simply allow us to maintain a certain level of existence that helps to keep all our systems functioning normally.

Routines require a minimum of effort. We hardly exert ourselves in accomplishing them. Indeed, we may complete a routine—like driving to the office or taking out the trash—hardly conscious of having exerted any energy or effort at all. Moreover, routines require little thought. They take no planning, require no serious monitoring or evaluation, and are done most of the time almost without thinking. In fact, much of the time we are involved in routines, we are thinking about something else, as when someone listens to the radio while getting ready for the day or driving to the office. Routines cost us little more than time and inconvenience, which we willingly invest for the benefit we derive from observing them. And routines seldom change. We always drive to work the same way, follow the same order of activities in getting ready for the day or clean up the kitchen in the same manner after a meal. We have no sense of a need to change our routines, so we continue to follow them without much thought or adjustment day after day, year after year. And our routines serve us well, allowing us to maintain a certain status quo in different areas of our lives but not really helping us to advance in any of those areas.

A discipline is different. A discipline is something to which we submit in order to effect change. As Dallas Willard says, "A discipline is any activity within our power that we engage in to enable us to do what we cannot do by direct effort,"[1] like losing weight or getting in shape (so that we'll look and feel better and live longer), or learning a new skill on the job (so that we can secure a promotion, raise or better position). We can't make ourselves feel better, and we can't achieve a promotion or raise on our own, so we submit to certain disciplines that we believe will enable us to accomplish those things not immediately within our power.

Disciplines can require a great deal of effort. We push our bodies to new levels of exertion as we go through our daily workout, or we stretch our minds in new directions to understand some new procedure or master some new technology. We force our brains and bodies into concentrated, strenuous activity in order to prepare ourselves for taking on new roles or responsibilities or assuming a new lifestyle. A good discipline requires serious intellectual involvement—in planning, monitoring progress, evaluating levels of mastery and so forth.

Further, disciplines tend to involve significant investments of time. To do them we have to sacrifice other activities we might otherwise choose to do and concentrate time and effort on mastering those disciplines that we hope will get us what we want. We have to be willing to give up certain things we enjoy—foods, leisure activities or rest—in order to devote the time and effort needed for getting in shape, becoming a better worker or preparing for a new job. And disciplines tend to get adjusted from time to time. As we reach one level of expertise or mastery, we may alter our disciplines in order to push beyond that level to a still higher one.

Both routines and disciplines are important in our lives. Yet they are clearly not the same. A problem arises when we allow what are intended to be disciplines to become mere routines—like my summer workouts. When that happens, not only do our disciplines not produce the desired results, but they become tedious, boring and dull. We may be faithful in attending to them, but not in the way they were designed and certainly without much in the way of results to show for our effort.

This problem is especially serious in the area of our spiritual lives when our practice of the disciplines of grace is allowed to become a mere spiritual routine instead.

God has given us the disciplines of grace as means to help us grow in love for him and our neighbors. These precious tools—prayer, the Word of God, worship, solitude, giving, fasting, silence in God's presence and so forth—bring us into his presence in ways that everyday living does not, enabling us to glimpse his glory and tap into his power for daily renewal in Christ. But when our practice of the disciplines of grace is allowed to lapse into routine devotional activities—when our disciplines become mere routines—they lose their power to bring us face to face with the Lord in life-transforming ways.

In Jesus' day no group of people was more renowned for their discipline than the Jewish religious leaders. One and all knew them as the men who prayed the most, knew Scripture the best, fasted the most consistently and gave the most alms to the poor. Some of them were sincerely spiritual, even godly persons, such as Zacharias and Nicodemus. Yet, for a great many of them, their disciplines had not served to prepare their hearts for the coming of the Messiah or for being able to recognize him when he appeared among them teaching and doing good. Their practice of the disciplines of grace had not helped them grow in love, either for God or their neighbors. Many of them were proud, greedy, scornful of the ignorant masses and protective of their special status in society. They saw Jesus as a threat and, after putting up with him for three years, conspired to put him to death.

All their disciplines had been of no use in helping them to experience God's glory and enter into his grace. They pursued their practice of spiritual disciplines merely in order to keep their place in society rather than to grow in the grace and knowledge of the Lord. Their disciplines had become mere routines, giving them a certain amount of self-satisfaction and enabling them to preserve their status in the eyes of the people; yet their spiritual lives were empty and devoid of any real relationship with God. They had become "whitewashed tombs," as Jesus observed—self-satisfied, self-righteous, complacent and smug.

Before our own spiritual lives degenerate into such a condition and we become negative and judgmental, lacking in compassion and having little zeal for the life of faith or the mission of Christ, we need to consider whether our own use of the disciplines of grace is according to God's purpose and plan.

### The State of Spiritual Disciplines Today

In the church today we are blessed with abundant resources and given endless advice and encouragement for using the disciplines of grace for Christ and his kingdom. There is no shortage of Bibles and Bible study materials, groups and classes for learning the Word of God, books and conferences on prayer, manuals concerning and opportunities for worship, or calls for fasting. Most people I know who profess to be followers of Christ are engaged in spiritual disciplines at some level, although many of them will at the same time admit to a certain lack of satisfaction with their devotional lives. On the whole, though, it would seem that the practice of spiritual disciplines is alive and relatively well among the members of the church.

But the question arises as to why the church appears to be so lacking in power. Why do our biblical convictions play so meager a role in shaping our culture and giving direction to our society? Why are the ranks of churches declining as a percentage of the population as a whole—in spite of the megachurch phenomenon? Why do such behaviors as incivility, vulgarity and indecency continue to rise and be tolerated in our society? Why are believers in general so reticent about their faith? Why do we expend so much effort in squabbles over such matters as forms of worship, the role of women in the church and the place of Christian pop culture in the life of the community of faith? Why are we so despised by the cultural and social elite of our society? And why, when we disperse throughout society as the leaven of Christ's kingdom in the loaf of a sinful and dying age, are we so indistinct as citizens of the heavenly realm?

There are doubtless many answers to such questions, but one suggests itself to me that, from my own experience and observations, as well as my reading and study, requires further examination. That is, as a community, believers are not experiencing what God intends for them from their practice of the disciplines of grace. As Simon Chan suggests in the earlier quote, either we are not involved in spiritual disciplines or our involvement has become perfunctory and not a source of grace and glory for transformed living. It is possible that many have allowed their spiritual disciplines to lapse into mere routines without being aware. They are praying, reading their Bibles and faithfully attending worship services, but nothing much is happening in their lives as citizens of the kingdom of God. They continue to be strapped with the same besetting sins, seem hardly more inclined to offer themselves in sacrificial service to the Lord, are quick to criticize and condemn those who disagree with them on spiritual matters, and are reluctant to engage their neighbors in spiritual conversations for the cause of the gospel. At the same time they are active in the disciplines of grace—having their daily devotions, being in a study group, faithfully attending at worship—but they are not growing in grace. Rather, they are barely managing to maintain a kind of spiritual status quo amid the press of temptations, duties and the hectic pace of postmodern society.

For such people it may well be that their spiritual disciplines have become mere routines, without power and effect for turning the world upside down for Christ.

What God intended as disciplines to bring us into the presence of his glory and to transform us increasingly into the image of his Son have, for many of us, become mere routines—mindless, effortless, fruitless undertakings that placate our sense of duty but do nothing to equip us for kingdom living in the world.

### In the Arena of Grace

The disciplines of grace constitute a special arena of grace in which, through intensive personal encounter with the living God, in the presence of his Spirit and the power of his Word, our love for him is renewed and deepened, and we are further enlivened in Christ to love our neighbors as ourselves. This is not to say that we do not meet Christ at other times in our lives or that God is not to be found throughout the course of our day as he makes himself known through the world around us or guides and prompts us by his Spirit. It is simply to insist that, in the disciplines of grace, there is an intensification of God's presence and power that comes from careful and deliberate attention to these disciplines, and that can effect dramatic and permanent change in our lives. This experience of the transforming grace of God cannot be found anywhere else. Without it we can hardly expect to know the life-changing power of Christ in the normal course of our lives.

What happens in the practice of spiritual disciplines? How should we enter into them, and what might we expect as a result? In 2 Corinthians 3:12-18 the apostle Paul shows us what God intends should happen during the practice of the spiritual discipline of God's Word. What we discover here is equally valid for all the spiritual disciplines:

> Therefore, having such a hope, let us be very bold, and not like Moses, who put a veil over his face so that the sons of Israel might not continually look upon that which was fading away. But their minds were hardened, for until this very day the same veil remains at the reading of the Old Covenant. It has not been removed. Because it is done away with in Christ. But until this day, whenever Moses is read, a veil remains over their hearts. But when someone turns to the Lord, the veil is removed. And the Lord is the Spirit; and wherever the Spirit of the Lord is—liberty! But we all, with our faces unveiled, as we behold the glory of the Lord, are being transformed into that same image from glory to glory, even as from the Lord, the Spirit (my translation).

Notice first of all that spiritual disciplines are arenas of grace in which we encounter a special concentration of the power of God's Spirit and of his Word. God's Word prescribes the spiritual disciplines, and his Spirit provides the power enabling us to benefit from the disciplines prescribed in his Word (we shall examine this more carefully in the next chapter). These two powers, present in all the spiritual disciplines, are at work in our lives according to God's good pleasure for each one of us (Phil 2:12-13), that is, according to our individual needs and the opportunities for ministry that God places before us each day.

In anticipation of entering these arenas where the powers of God are especially concentrated for our growth, we look forward in faith eagerly to what the Lord might do in our lives. Our attitude is like that of the psalmist who prayed, "Open thou mine eyes, that I may behold wondrous things out of thy law" (Ps 119:18), or like David when he came before the Lord saying, "Hear me when I call, O God of my righteousness: thou hast enlarged me *when I was* in my distress; have mercy upon me, and hear my prayer" (Ps 4:1). A sense of eagerness and heightened expectation settles on us as we enter by faith into the practice of spiritual disciplines. Like Moses ascending Mt. Sinai, we experience a feeling of wonder, excitement and fear at the prospect of meeting with the living God. And we do have faith that we shall meet with him, shall "look full in his wonderful face" and hear him speaking directly to us, have audience with him concerning the desires of our heart, and be warmed and renewed by his love and instructed by his Word. Our joy in this privilege and in our love for him who provides it for us begins to rise and revive as we enter the arena of his power to encounter him afresh. Like children rushing downstairs on Christmas morning, we are filled with wonder, excitement and the prospect of blessing and delight.

Once there we encounter the glory of God, that is, the very presence of God as he makes himself known through one or more means, assuring us of his presence with us and enveloping us in his grace.[2] Paul tells us that the glory of God comes off the pages of Scripture—or fills the atmosphere of our prayers or any of the other spiritual disciplines—and we are suddenly aware of a loving, other-worldly power making itself known to us, affecting us heart, soul, mind and strength. We see God in new ways, experience him more profoundly and really *hear* him speaking with us by his Word and Spirit, feel his comforting or convicting presence with greater intensity and passion, and desire to draw closer to him. With Moses we plead, "Lord, show me your glory!" We know what Jeremiah experienced when he exulted, "Thy words were found, and I did eat them; and thy word was unto me the joy and rejoicing of mine heart" (Jer 15:16). Our bodies may be affected by such an encounter with the living God. We may raise our hands in praise or supplication, weep tears of joy and gladness or sorrow for our sins. We may cover our faces in shame, cry out in joy or burst into a song of praise and thanks to God. Our hearts may race with the prospect of new growth or opportunities for serving the Lord. We may find our minds transfixed for long moments on a phrase from God's Word or some aspect of his creation that reveals his beauty and glory in a new and wondrous way. We may fall to our knees or leap to our feet. Or we may simply sit in stunned silence and marvel at the grace of God for sinners such as we. We feel ourselves, whether slowly or suddenly, being drawn beyond our present condition to a greater sense of Christlikeness, a deeper love for him and stronger desire to show his love to others. Like the disciples on the Mount of Transfiguration we would prolong this experience of the glory of God, for there is nothing in this world that can compare with it.

But this manifestation of the glory of God—whatever form it takes—is not merely for the purpose of exciting, soothing or stimulating us during the practice of spiritual disciplines. Rather, it is given to transform us increasingly into the image of the Lord. The Spirit of God, says Paul, takes the manifestation of God's glory that we encounter in the practice of spiritual disciplines and brings it to bear on our lives to make us more like Jesus Christ. From one experience of God's glory to the next, we see new aspects of his nature that we long to possess in ourselves. Our own sins are illuminated with such brilliance that we come to hate them and love the righteousness of the Lord more and more. We discover new ways that we might lay down our lives for our friends, reach out to our lost neighbors or show the love of Christ to members of our family or church. A new resolve begins to form in our hearts. Old selfish thoughts and ways are despised and rejected. Definite plans take shape by which we will act on what God has shown us, and we become aware of a new power at work within us, preparing us to live for Christ in new and exciting ways. Hope, confidence and joy rise, and we are thrilled with the prospect of going forth to live for Christ in whatever he may bring our way this day. Even in those "dark nights of the soul" we will know the comforting presence and grace of God assuring us that his love is surrounding us and that he will never fail nor forsake us (Ps 13; 43).

So the outcome of spiritual disciplines is that we become more like Jesus—him increasing in us and our selfish, sinful ways declining more and more. Or, as Jonathan Edwards put it:

> In the renewing and sanctifying work of the Holy Ghost, those things are wrought in the soul that are above nature, and of which there is nothing of the like kind in the soul by nature; and they are caused to exist in the soul

habitually, and according to such a stated constitution or law that lays
such a foundation for exercises in a continued course as is called a principle of nature. Not only are remaining principles assisted to do their work
more freely and fully, but those principles are restored that were utterly
destroyed by the fall; and the mind thenceforward habitually exerts those
acts that the dominion of sin had made it as wholly destitute of as a dead
body is of vital acts.[3]

In other words, we grow beyond ourselves to become more like our
Savior and King. Not in huge leaps and bounds but slowly and gradually—and certainly. We become affected with a greater love for God as
well as for our neighbors. Our lives take on more of a sense of mission.
We find that we are more willing to sacrifice for others and that we are
bolder and more consistent in talking with them about the Lord. Increasingly the concerns of this world "grow strangely dim/In the light of his
glory and grace." Again, Edwards on the effect of encountering the glory
and power of God in the disciplines of grace:

> But this light, as it reaches the bottom of the heart, and changes the
> nature, so it will effectually dispose to a universal obedience. It shows God
> as worthy to be obeyed and served. It draws forth the heart in a sincere
> love to God, which is the only principle of a true, gracious, and universal
> obedience; and it convinces of the reality of those glorious rewards that
> God has promised to them that obey him.[4]

Thus our mighty God works in and on us in these special arenas of
grace to show himself to us more clearly and make us fitter vessels for
bearing his truth and love to a grace-starved world. Granted, our experience in the disciplines of grace may not always be full and exhilarating;
however, we believe it can be, and we desire that it should be. But where
spiritual disciplines are lacking, or where they have been allowed to
become routines in our lives, little such experience and few such effects
are in evidence. Instead a kind of spiritual stagnancy sets in that can
become a breeding ground for self-satisfaction, self-righteousness, com-
placency and smugness in the life of faith.

### Routines or Disciplines?
How can we know when our practice of spiritual disciplines has
degenerated into mere routine?

Here are four questions you can use to assess the state of your spiritual disciplines. Using these questions frequently and honestly helps keep me in that special arena of grace so that my spiritual disciplines are better able to accomplish what they are intended for and so that they do not lapse into mere routines instead. When they do, I can become aware of it quickly and take steps to recover a right use of the disciplines of grace.

*What are my motives as I enter the disciplines of grace?* Why are you undertaking this activity? Are you motivated by love for God and a desire to meet with him face to face? Do you long to grow in grace? Are you coming in faith, in the promise that God will meet with you, show you his glory and transform you into the very image of Christ? Are you eager to know more of the love of Christ for the people around you?

Or are you spending your time in Bible reading, prayer or any of the other spiritual disciplines just because you feel like you should? Do you have one eye on the clock as you begin? Do you (if only subconsciously) begrudge this time you have set apart to be with the Lord, and are you thinking of a dozen other things you'd rather or should be doing? Are these spiritual exercises simply ways of assuring you that you're "a good Christian"? Do they keep you feeling somehow superior to those around you who do not pray or spend time in God's Word? Do you embark upon these practices looking for something to teach someone else, seeking to justify some behavior or sentiment of your own, concerned only about your own personal interests or needs, or determined to discover how someone else is wrong about this, that or the other? What is your motivation in entering into the disciplines of grace?

Do not assume that you can answer this question of motivation without some careful and critical thought, and a great deal of soul-searching before the Lord. The starting point of Christian growth is knowing where we need to grow, seeing areas of our lives where change is due, and accepting the fact that we are not where we ought or would like to be. Be honest in your self-examination. Commit to a season of prayer using these questions as your guide. Wait upon the Lord to show you the motives of your heart as you assess the state of your spiritual disciplines. If any of the answers to the questions I've asked are disturbing, take them to the Lord in prayer, calling upon him to renew your motives for submitting to the disciplines of grace and to make them what they ought to be. Only faith in the Lord and eager expectation of meeting with him will suffice as motives for submitting to the disciplines of grace. *How well do I understand the disciplines of grace?* Do you know what you're doing here? Do you really understand how to read and study the Bible? To pray? To fast before the Lord, enter into a season of solitude or make offerings acceptable to him? Is your involvement in the fellowship of God's saints what it ought to be? Do you really understand what worship is all about? Are your spiritual disciplines as complete and thorough as they ought to be? Or are you content merely to go through the same familiar and comfortable routines without being stretched in new ways?

There is room for us to grow—and plenty of help as well[5]—when it comes to getting a better handle on the disciplines of grace. None of us has or ever will master any of the spiritual disciplines. The best we can hope for is to keep improving in our understanding and use of them, and this requires an unswerving commitment to learn more about them and to put to use what we are learning as best we can. Do you have this kind of attitude toward the disciplines? If not, you may already be stuck in mere routines.

*What is my experience in the disciplines of grace?* Is your experience in spiritual disciplines the kind described above—intellectually active, emotionally charged, spiritually profound and enlivening, reflective and introspective, determined on change, but resting in the grace and presence of the Lord at all times? Or is your involvement in spiritual disciplines dry, tedious, unexciting, lacking in affections—a mere going through the motions rather than an encounter with the living God? Do you sense the presence of God's glory in the midst of spiritual disciplines? Or are you merely reading or mouthing words in an unemotional, unconvicted and unconvincing manner? Are you communing with the living God or just going through a prayer list? Is your mind fixed and alert, or does it wander to other more interesting or pressing subjects? Are you beholding the glory of God or just preparing for some Bible study? Are you being stabbed to the heart in the depths of your being, lifted to heights of joy and confidence, imbued with new power and fixed on new resolves—or just knocking off another activity on your things-to-do list?

Every indication in Scripture—from the experiences of people like Moses and Hannah to the testimonies of the psalmists and the recollections of the apostles—is that being in the presence of God can affect us powerfully. We all know seasons of spiritual depression when we can't work up much enthusiasm about being with the Lord or when life is just too great a weight to bear. Because of this, our practice of the disciplines of grace goes up and down; yet we may expect the practice of spiritual disciplines to be more consistently satisfying and powerful. We should desire our involvement in the disciplines of grace to bring us to the kind of heights of spiritual sensitivity as expressed in these stanzas from the hymn "More About Jesus Would I Know":

> More about Jesus; in his Word, holding communion with my Lord;
> hearing his voice in ev'ry line, making each faithful saying mine.
> More, more about Jesus, more, more about Jesus,
> more of his saving fullness see, more of his love Who died for me.
> More about Jesus on his throne, riches in glory all his own;
> more of his kingdom's sure increase; more of his coming, Prince of Peace!
> More, more about Jesus, more, more about Jesus,
> more of his saving fullness see, more of his love Who died for me.[6]

Communing with him. Hearing him. Embracing his truth. Seeing his glory. Expanding your vision of his reign. Desiring him more. Advancing his kingdom. We have every reason and right to expect that our experience of him in the disciplines of grace will be as pronounced and profound as this. If it is not, then it may be time for adjusting our disciplines in order to get back on the rails of spiritual growth once again.

*What is happening in my life as a result of the disciplines of grace?* Can you point to specific times when God has spoken so plainly that your life was truly changed? Have you known the searching power of his Spirit as he exposes some besetting sin, and have you begun to find the grace to overcome it? Can you say that you have grown in love for the Lord over the past several years, and in what ways? Has your involvement in spiritual disciplines been a source of power for witness or more actively loving others?

Disciplines that do not produce growth are not disciplines at all. Rather, like my summer workouts, they have become mere routines, done to satisfy some sense of "oughtness" or duty but with little sanctifying effect. God has given us the disciplines of grace so that, as we are exposed to his glory from one encounter to the next, we will be progressively transformed into the very image of Jesus Christ, and, being transformed, nothing and no one we encounter will remain the same. Wherever Jesus went, at least one thing can be said of him: we have no record of anyone responding to him with indifference. His life and teachings demanded response, bringing people to the point of change or stiffening their resolve to live in sin. When we are growing in the grace and knowledge of the Lord, our lives will be similarly charged. People will know where we stand, will see the Lord Jesus in our actions and hear him in our words, and be left with a choice to make as to where they will stand with him.

That this sort of thing is happening so rarely among the members of the Christian community should lead each of us to consider carefully whether our practice of the disciplines of grace is having the effect that God intends. And should we discover that our spiritual disciplines have slipped—or have the tendency to slip—to the level of mere routines, then we may begin the hard and happy work of rediscovering the grace of God and the power of his presence all over again. Moving from routine to renewal in the disciplines of grace will not ensure a life of uninterrupted joy and power; many other factors come into play as well. However, a proper use of the disciplines of grace can be a starting point for renewal for those whose lives seem to be on hold with the Lord and who are eager to begin growing in his grace again.

### Questions for Study or Discussion

1. How would you describe your own experience of the disciplines of grace? What kinds of adjectives, descriptive phrases or analogies come to mind?

2. In the experience of most Christians some lapsing of our disciplines into mere routines from time to time is inevitable. Why do you think this happens? What might be some indicators to suggest that this was beginning to happen in your case?

3. Look again at the description of being in the arena of God's grace, that is, practicing spiritual disciplines as God intends. Which aspects would you like to know more of in your practice of the disciplines of grace? What do you think may be keeping you from that experience?

4. Spiritual disciplines are intended to lead us to growth in grace. In what specific ways can you see that your practice of the disciplines of

grace has brought about real change into Christlikeness in your life recently? In which areas of your life would you like to know more growth and change?

5. What would you like to see happen in your life as a result of this study of the disciplines of grace? What goals will you set? How will you be able to tell at the end of this study that you have begun to know more of the disciplines of grace and less of the routines?

# 2

# the powers of god & the disciplines of grace

*True theology arises from personal experience of God in Jesus Christ,*
*and reflecting on that experience leads to a deeper experiential knowledge of God.*
*The one who is engaged in "an exact tracing of the glory of God" will be*
*affected by that glory, which inevitably elicits praise.*
SIMON CHAN

*Take my yoke upon you, and learn of me . . . and ye shall find rest*
*unto your souls.*
MATTHEW 11:29

*I*'m not a collector, but if I were, I would probably collect tops. I have always been fascinated by tops. As a child I would spin them for hours at a time, marveling at the mysterious power that kept them standing on end in defiance of the law of gravity. During recess at school I would often snatch a jack away from the girls and head off to some remote corner of the asphalt to spin the little wonder while my friends played kickball or tag. Only as I began to study science in school did I learn about centrifugal force and how it worked to overcome the law of gravity and allow a top to thrill me with a few moments of fascination and delight.

Recently I saw what has to be the quintessential top. I was in a science store at the mall, browsing while my wife shopped elsewhere, and I saw a cast-iron top lying on a piece of acrylic plastic, which served as the cover of a wooden block about half the size of a brick. I could not resist the desire to spin that top and watch it whirl in apparent defiance of the laws of nature. I was not able to get it going, however, and one of the store clerks came over and asked, "Would you like me to do that for you?"

After looking around to make sure I didn't see anyone I knew, I said, "Sure." He gave that little top a good lick, and it began to dance obediently like a dervish on that piece of acrylic. Then he grasped the plastic sheet with the first fingers and thumbs of his two hands, lifted it about four inches off the block of wood, and pulled it rapidly out from under the top. Whereupon the top spun gaily *in mid-air!* I could not believe my eyes, and when after some minutes it finally fell to the surface of the wooden block, I said, "Do that again!" Which the clerk obligingly did, much to my wonder and delight.

Then it hit me. Buried in that wooden block was a strong magnet, one of its poles turned toward the same pole in the top, and the force of magnetism was repelling the top, suspending it in the air, while the centrifugal force generated by the clerk's spin kept it humming obediently above the block of wood.

Two unseen but very strong powers. Magnets can generate so much force that they are used to lift tons of scrap iron, while every trucker knows the power of centrifugal force to turn an eighteen-wheeler on its side on an expressway exit ramp. You can't see either of these powers. You can't feel, taste or hold them in your hand. But they are real, and the power they can exert earns the respect and appreciation of all those who work with them daily.

In the same way two unseen but very powerful forces are at work for us in the spiritual disciplines. You can't see them, and you might be tempted at times to think that they're not really there. In the practice of the disciplines of grace, God's Word and Spirit are waiting to enable us to enter into God's glory in life-changing ways.

We have said that spiritual disciplines are special arenas of grace in which, through intensive, personal encounter with the living God, in the presence of his Spirit and the power of his Word, our love for him is renewed and deepened, and we are further enlivened in Christ to love our neighbors as ourselves. What makes spiritual disciplines so powerful to effect change unto Christlikeness in our lives is the presence of God's Spirit and his Word in each of them. Certainly God's Word and Spirit are with those who love him at all times. But as we enter into the disciplines of grace, with the right motives and an attentive spirit, seeking the end of a transformed life, those two powers operate in unseen, supernatural ways to overcome the law of sin that persists in our hearts, the bad habits we have accumulated over the years, and our want of experience in the life of faith to make us new people in Christ Jesus. The powers of God—his Spirit and Word—make the disciplines of grace a vital aspect of our lives in Christ, as there the glory of God works to change us increasingly into the likeness of the Lord.

But those powers are not accessible to us in mere mindless, effortless, pointless routines. Only as we recover the use of spiritual disciplines as God intends them will we be able to benefit from the power of his Word and Spirit at work in our lives.

### Understanding Spiritual Disciplines

In the last chapter I remarked on the importance of making certain that we understand the nature of spiritual disciplines and of each of the disciplines in particular in order to gain the most benefit from our involvement with them. Let's examine more closely the definition of spiritual disciplines that I have mentioned twice now.

*Special arenas of grace.* The Christian life is an excursion on a river of grace, as the psalmist observed: *"There is* a river, the streams whereof shall make glad the city of God, the holy *place* of the tabernacles of the most High"* (Ps 46:4). En route to our heavenly destination we are buoyed up by the constantly flowing, ever-fresh grace of the Lord, sustaining and providing for us among whom he has come to make his dwelling. Our journey is not always smooth. There are rapids and sharp turns to negotiate, many distractions along the shore to draw us off course, places where the water is dangerously shallow and we may run aground, and unseen obstacles embedded in the river bottom. In order to negotiate our journey with a minimum of disruption and damage, we need to mark the deepest and best channels of the river of grace, those special places where the current flows swiftest and safest, so that we might move successfully each day to the next place on our journey.

Not long ago I stood on the bank of the Mississippi River in West

Memphis, Arkansas, and watched as a tugboat captain negotiated a sharp turn at a narrow place in the river and brought his eighteen barges safely through to calmer water. Even from my place on the bank it was clear that he was an experienced riverboat captain who knew how to use the river channel to his advantage. Employing his engines with great skill and care, he nudged his barges to port, turning and pointing them so that they would come into the central channel. Then, letting the river do most of the work, he kept his vessel and its barges dead center in the rapidly flowing channel, deftly avoiding the shallows on either side and the many tree trunks that were sticking out from the river bed, until he came safely into straighter, smoother passage south of where I stood. That captain knew the special places in the mighty river where he had to resort in order to complete his journey with the greatest success and ease, and he worked hard to make the most of that deep water.

The spiritual disciplines are like those deep, swift-flowing channels. They constitute an opportunity for coming into the grace of God in greater depth, with greater passion and greater effect than we experience in the normal course of our everyday lives. Avoid them, or use them in a careless manner, and we will end up aground in life, buffeted by obstacles and frustrated in our journey with the Lord. But understand those deep channels, learn to negotiate that swift-flowing water and stick to them as often as possible, and your voyage on the river of grace will be much smoother, much more satisfying, and you will be carried along by much more power.

*Intensive, personal encounter with the living God.* From time to time we all fall into the trap of allowing our spiritual disciplines to become ends in themselves. Our time in God's Word finds us getting through two chapters a day, finishing a lesson in a study guide or working through some daily devotional material. Our prayer time is mainly employed in completing a prayer list of all the subjects in whatever formula or guide we follow. Worship becomes little more than a time for seeing our Christian friends and hoping for some blessing from the Lord to prepare us for the week ahead.

When these become our primary motivations and attitudes in the disciplines of grace, we are well on our way to seeing them become mere routines. God's purpose in the spiritual disciplines is that we should come into an intensive, personal encounter with him. The disciplines are the vehicles by which we enter into that encounter; they are not the encounter itself.

In each of the spiritual disciplines our purpose must be to meet with God. For us to realize this purpose, our approach must be intensive. This may mean, first of all, that we need to find a place and a time to meet with the Lord when distractions will be at a minimum. This is perhaps why so many of the saints of Scripture seem to have preferred the early morning. Abraham appears to have kept a special place and time—just about daybreak—when he would go to meet the Lord (Gen 19:27). David said, "My voice shalt thou hear in the morning, O LORD" (Ps 5:3). Jesus often arose before the light of day to capture intensive, undistracted time with his Father (Mk 1:35). By having a special place and time to meet the Lord, when distractions and disruptions can be kept at a minimum, we will more likely realize the purpose of spiritual disciplines.

Moreover, intensive meetings require sufficient time. They cannot be accomplished on the run. Suppose you needed to talk to your spouse about a very pressing matter, and all he or she could do was listen while reading the paper, preparing the evening meal or getting ready to go somewhere else. You would hardly feel as though your pressing concern was being given the intensive attention that it deserved. The same is true with the time we set aside for spiritual disciplines. This time must be kept in reserve, guarded fiercely and entered into with undivided attention if those disciplines are going to bring us into the presence of the living God and the power of his Word and Spirit.

Intensive meetings are also of such importance that it is wise to keep some record of them, so that we may follow through as our time with the Lord indicates. During my tenure as president of Chesapeake Theological Seminary, I would often have occasion to meet intensively with staff, faculty or students. Having set aside the time for the meeting, ensuring that there would be no distractions or unnecessary disruptions to divert our attention from the business at hand, I would make notes of our conversation, reviewing them with whomever I was meeting before we parted, and then setting them down in a follow-up memo that would serve as a basis for our carrying through on the items we had decided.

Something like this needs to happen in our spiritual disciplines. As God reveals himself to us in his Word or communes with us in solitude, fasting or prayer, we need to make sure not only that we're paying careful attention and communing with him concerning what he is saying to us but that we record our experience in some manner that will better ensure our ability to carry out what we have heard. I like to keep a daily journal in which I reflect, in a few words, on what the Lord has taught me in my time of Bible reading or how he has spoken to my heart as I have communed with him in prayer. This becomes a record that I can review and resort to, both for that day and the days to come, as I work to carry out what God has shown me in our time together. Sharing what we have learned with a close friend or spouse can help to impress it more deeply on us as my wife, Susie, and I have often found in sharing with one another from our devotional journals. Others have found writing poetry to be a wonderful and memorable way of imprinting their hearts and minds with what God has shown them in those intensive times of communion with him in the disciplines of grace.[1]

In addition to being intensive, our time in the disciplines of grace must also be personal. Do not let your spiritual disciplines become time invested primarily for someone else, time when you search the Scriptures for answers to their questions, or when your prayers are predominantly given over to other people's needs. Certainly these concerns will be part of the practice of spiritual disciplines. But spiritual disciplines are intended mainly to benefit us, to massage the grace of God more deeply into our hearts, minds and lives, and they cannot do that unless a significant portion of the intensive time we spend with the Lord is given to personal needs and concerns.

The disciplines of grace are uniquely designed to bring us personally into the presence of God. I have found this to be true in praying the psalms. The psalms give me great freedom to be myself before the Lord. Using words God has provided, I may confess my sins (Ps 32; 38; 51), get angry at the wicked (Ps 83; 137), weep and intercede for persecuted brethren (Ps 14; 31), call down God's wrath against spiritual foes (Ps 43; 74), exult in his goodness (Ps 103; 139), unabashedly and boldly claim his promises (Ps 80; 85) and set my goals and ambitions before him (Ps 40; 90), all without fear of being rejected or condemned. In other words, I can be myself with the Lord, not playing games, not refusing to look at areas of personal wretchedness and sin, not denying the wonderful things the Lord says concerning his tender love for me. This then carries over into all the other disciplines of grace and helps to make each of them a truly personal encounter with the living God as well.

I find that the more careful I am to make my practice of the disciplines of grace as intensive and personal as they can be, the more they bring me into the very presence of the living God, deepening my love for him and showing me ways that I can better love my neighbor as myself.

One morning not long ago my daily reading of God's Word found me in 1 Chronicles 14, where David inquired as to whether or not he should make a frontal assault on the Philistines (vv. 8-17). Instead the Lord told him to wait until he heard "the sound of marching in the tops of the balsam trees" (NIV), then to come around behind the Philistines and attack, which David did with complete success.

I was immediately reminded of the story of Elisha and his servant, when the prophet asked God to draw back the veil of eternity and show his servant that, the Syrian threat notwithstanding, the hosts of God stood ready to their defense (2 Kings 6:8-19). My time of prayer in the psalms led me to meditate on the many promises of angelic protection that we find therein (Ps 34:7; 91:11). I made a note in my journal of thanks to God for the help of his heavenly hosts that he provides us with each day.

That afternoon I took a few moments for some time alone with the Lord to contemplate his beauty and wonder at his glory in the creation around our home. It was a warm and windy day. As I sat on the porch, gusts of wind were tearing through the poplar trees on a nearby hill, and the sound it made was like the moving of a great company. I recalled my morning devotions and wondered to myself, half-facetiously, where those angelic hosts might be hastening to. On what great mission had they been sent? Which demonic scheme were they marching off to thwart, and what important saint might know their rescue on that glorious day?

Just then a gust of wind rushed across our porch, blowing my hair around with such a frenzy that it actually stung my forehead. Suddenly I experienced both the shame of rebuke and the thrill of God's presence. I thought, *I'm the object of that marching host! I'm the mission on which they have been sent. It's to my care and well-being that they have been dispatched!* I was so thrilled with the lengths to which the Lord goes for the care of his people that I burst into a song of praise to the Lord right there and then.

Later that evening, as I was reflecting back on the day, I wanted to record my experience so that I could reflect on it more fully. I was able to do so in the following sonnet:

> *I Heard the Sound of Armies Marching*
> 1 Chronicles 14:15, 2 Kings 6:15-17
>
> I heard the sound of armies marching through
> the poplar trees, where earth and heaven meet.
> The breeze-bent boughs betrayed the unseen feet
> of vast, unnumbered hosts, who rushed to do
> the bidding of the Lord, beyond the view
> of earth-bound men. I knew it was the beat
> of countless angels' wings, and rose to greet
> them as they passed. Oh how I wished I knew
> their mission! What revolt would they subdue?
> What rescue undertake? What mighty feat
> essay against dark forces? What complete
> and glorious victory would soon ensue?
> And then I saw, wind whipping through my hair,
> their ranks deployed around me, everywhere.

One week later I was visiting with a pastor who was struggling to discern God's leading in his life and that of his congregation. They were under tremendous pressure to decide whether to stay in their present denomination, where they felt their ministry was being stifled, or move to a new one, as well as what the best timing might be for doing so. Because of the growing pressure for a decision, John was tempted to do something hasty and expedient just to get the matter behind them. But what he really wanted to do—and what he knew he should do—was wait on the Lord until his Spirit should make clear to all which course they should follow. The temptation to do something, anything, was great, but he felt strongly that they should wait for the clear leading of the Lord.

As we talked, it was clear that John was bearing a heavy burden as the shepherd of his flock. He wanted to know the Lord's will, but he wanted equally to get the whole thing over with, one way or another. How would he ever be able to know what was the right course to take? I shared with him my meditation on David's waiting for the Lord's specific leading and my experience of being reminded of God's presence and care. I encouraged him not to act until the Lord made abundantly clear which way the Spirit was blowing and the armies of the Lord were marching in his life. He was encouraged and relieved, and resolved not to act until he and his congregation could plainly discern the leading of the Spirit of God together.

I am sure I will never forget either the intensity or the deeply personal nature of that combination of encounters with the living God, or of the way that God used something he showed me for my life as a means of ministry to someone else.

*The presence of God's Spirit and Word.* Because spiritual disciplines are principally arenas for encountering God's Spirit and Word in intensely personal ways, we need to develop patience and discernment to wait upon the Lord as he communes with us. How easy it is to read blithely over familiar passages of Scripture, thinking that we already know what this text is about, or to prattle on in prayer in a one-way monologue before the throne of grace, never pausing to listen, reflect or respond to the still, small voice of God. How easy it is, in other words, to come into the practice of spiritual disciplines with our own agenda. I need to get through this morning devotional, cover my daily prayer list, sit through worship hoping to get something out of it and so forth. Such an attitude toward the disciplines of grace should tell us that we have lapsed into mere routine in our time with the Lord.

What should we expect in the presence of the Spirit and Word of God? Light to expose our sins and selfishness. Insight into God's truth at depths we have never experienced before. Startling new experiences of the glory and power of God. Renewed vision for a life of holiness, ministry and love. True, heartfelt compassion for the lost. A sharper sense of the magnitude of Jesus' offering, the perfection of his holiness, the majestic power of his reign and the certainty of his imminent return. Joy, fear, shame, exhilaration, thanksgiving, delight, unbounded hope. A sense of real, steady growth in the Lord, even in the face of adversity or trial. And, through it all, a constant awareness of the divine presence, comforting, encouraging, assuring, challenging, stimulating, prodding and cherishing us in the strong, undergirding arms of our Savior's love.

It is unreasonable to expect that this will always be our experience. Yet it can be, more and more. But it is difficult to realize such a presence of the Spirit and Word of God without being willing to wait upon the Lord, to listen carefully for his prompting, to open ourselves completely and without fear to his probing, prodding goads, and to dwell seriously and long on the content of our communion with him. To come away from the practice of spiritual disciplines with anything less than this is to miss the point of the disciplines altogether. We come into this special arena of grace not merely to complete some exercise of reading, talking or responding. We come to meet the living God, and we shall know beyond a shadow of a doubt that we have succeeded in that encounter when his glory envelops us in the ways we have summarized above. As Jonathan Edwards noted:

> Therefore, when the spirit that is at work amongst the people, tends this way, and brings many of them to high and exalting thoughts of the Divine Being, and his glorious perfections; and works in them an admiring, delightful sense of the excellency of Jesus Christ; representing him as the chief among ten thousand, and altogether lovely, and makes him precious to the soul; winning and drawing the heart with those motives and incitements to love, of which the apostle speaks. . . . The spirit that excites to love on these motives, and makes the attributes of God as revealed in the gospel, and manifested in Christ, delightful objects of contemplation; and makes the soul to long after God and Christ—after their presence and communion, acquaintance with them, and conformity to them—and to live so as to please and honour them, the spirit that quells contentions among men, and gives a spirit of peace and good will, excites to acts of outward kindness, and earnest desires of the salvation of souls—and causes a delight in those that appear as the children of God, and followers of Christ; I say, when a spirit operates after this manner among a people, there is the highest kind of evidence of the influence of a true and divine spirit.[2]

When this becomes our experience in the disciplines of grace more and more, we shall have no doubt about the fact that we have truly met in an intensive and personal way with the living and eternal God.

*Our love for him and for others is renewed and deepened.* Because chapter four is devoted to the question of the results that we should expect from the exercise of spiritual disciplines, I wish to touch on this matter only cursorily at this point, and that principally by warning of some unacceptable results.

### The Disciplines as Ends in Themselves

The end of our spiritual disciplines, as of all instruction in faith, is love, that is, that we may love God more with all our heart, mind and strength, and our neighbor as ourselves (1 Tim 1:5). Of what such love consists I shall have more to say later. For now, suffice it to observe that such love is not merely the dutiful completion of some devotional task.

It is very easy for our practice of spiritual disciplines to become mere routines, lacking much real thought, without intense and personal encounter with God, devoid of vital faith and producing few or no results in our lives. Indeed, every Christian who practices spiritual disciplines will lapse into this condition from time to time. Because we are sinful and weak, we can hardly avoid it. But we must resist the temptation of thinking that this is OK, that, after all, this is pretty much what everyone else I know experiences, and so this must be as good as it gets, and God must surely be at work here anyway, just as long as I am dutiful in going through the motions of the disciplines of grace. As Luder Whitlock has shown, this is to make the mistake of confusing the means of growth— the disciplines of grace—with the marks of maturity. He comments that the disciplines of grace "are the vehicles to help you reach spiritual maturity but must not be equated with it."[3] In other words, if all we have to show for our time spent in the disciplines of grace is a checkmark on a list—preparation for a Bible study, completing a daily devotion, getting through a prayer list, observing a fast—we have fallen far short of what God intends for us from immersing ourselves in these special arenas of grace.

This is to fall into the mindset of certain medieval theologians who used the sacraments of the church as instruments of congregational control, insisting that people come to worship and participate accordingly, whether they sensed any presence or blessing of the Lord or not. The formal term for such superficial adherence to sacramental routine is *opera operata*, or works that are effective as instruments of grace simply because we participate in them at some level. As Luther showed so powerfully, to settle for this view of worship, or any of the spiritual disciplines, is to minimize the role of faith and encounter with God and to exalt superficial works as that which above all else is pleasing to the Lord.[4]

While we must persevere at the disciplines of grace, even when we perceive that they have degenerated to mere routines, we must not be content with this situation but must seek to recover an active sense of the presence of God and to practice the disciplines in eager and expectant faith.[5] Without sincere and seeking faith in God, an eager expectation of meeting with him in life-changing ways, the disciplines of grace will avail us not a whit. However:

> Given this faith, there immediately follows the most precious affection of the heart, enlarging and deepening the human soul, that is, love as given by the Holy Spirit through faith in Christ. Thus the believer draws near to Christ, that loving and bounteous testator, and becomes a new and different man through and through.[6]

## The Disciplines as Sources of Knowledge Only

A second unacceptable result of the practice of spiritual disciplines is the mere accumulation of knowledge. While knowledge of God's Word and ways is essential to effective Christian living, such knowledge in and of itself can be harmful, even idolatrous. Such is the knowledge that the demons have of God. They can quote his Word freely and yet despise him all the while (Mt 4:1-11; Jas 2:19). Mere knowledge can make us prideful, leading us to look down on others who have not reached such lofty heights of intellectual insight (Jn 7:49; 1 Cor 8:1-3).[7] Knowledge by itself can even bring the wrath of God against us because we heap up truth without really applying it to our lives, thus missing the blessing that is intended, going away from spiritual disciplines unchanged and setting ourselves up for the Lord's chastening (Jn 13:17; Heb 12:5-11; Jas 1:22-25).

What Helmut Thielicke wrote concerning young theologians can be true of every one of us as well: "Young theologians manifest certain trumped-up intellectual effects which actually amount to nothing."[8] Mere knowledge, without a heart properly affected by the glory of the Lord and a life of consequent obedience, is of no eternal value and can be a source of great harm, to oneself as well as to others. How many times, over the course of nearly thirty years of ministry, have I seen well-meaning ministers and church leaders use Scripture as a rod of discipline to keep people in line with standard doctrinal positions or to categorize and condemn all who differ from them, with little expression of love or heartfelt pastoral concern? How often have I been guilty of this myself? This is what can happen when mere knowledge—knowledge without proper affections and obedience—becomes the end of our studies and our practice of the disciplines of grace. This kind of knowledge is less than useless. Thus we must take care in the practice of spiritual disciplines that we do not become content with mere knowledge as the result.

### The Disciplines for Others' Sake

Finally, we must not be content in the practice of spiritual disciplines if all we come out of them with are prescriptions for others. I have often encountered people who claim that God spoke to them during their prayers about something that I needed to do, or who wanted to share with me from their study of God's Word some truth that God had shown them, correcting or improving something I had said. People have pushed devotional literature at me, convinced that "you need to read this." And I have often made observations during my own practice of spiritual disciplines that I thought I should share with others in order to help or encourage them.

Some of this is good and useful. Indeed, if we love our neighbors as ourselves, we can hardly avoid seeing their needs and concerns coming to the surface during our seasons of communion with the Lord. But before we begin prescribing actions, changes in views or spiritual remedies for those around us, let us make certain that what God is making known to us in such times is first of all true of ourselves. Let us not overlook the log in our own eyes as we rush out to relieve others of the speck in theirs (Mt 7:1-5).

Further, as we contemplate sharing with others from the things God has shown us during our time with him to encourage, edify or correct them, let us make certain that we wait for the Lord to provide the opportunity and that we undertake such a mission in a heart of loving service. Nehemiah is an excellent example. Burdened about the situation in Jerusalem and knowing that he needed to seek the Persian king's help—that God had showed him in prayer what Artaxerxes needed to do—he was content to wait upon the Lord to open the door of opportunity and did not immediately rush into the king's chambers demanding an audience (Neh 1:4—2:8). When the opportunity did come, he did not lecture the king but entreated him graciously and reasonably, making himself available to serve as the king went about to do what God was guiding him to do.

Here are some excellent principles for sharing with others what God has shown us concerning them in our times of communion with him:

Wait for them to create a door of opportunity. Show them all due respect, honor and love. Be available to serve in order to help them fulfill what God has shown you concerning them. It is inevitable that God will speak to us concerning others as we practice the disciplines of grace in his presence. And, while this must not be our primary concern at such times, when it does result, we can realize the goal of spiritual disciplines by keeping these simple guidelines in mind as we go to share with others. By so doing we show, in a very real sense, that we have grown in love for others and not just as a dispenser of spiritual remedies or a huckster of theological advice. Here it is good to keep in mind Luther's dictum "The Christian is the slave of no man, but the servant of all."[9] As we may not submit in slavish obedience to any human being, so we must not seek to use our practice of the disciplines of grace as a pretense for enslaving others. Rather, we must always strive to ensure that what God shows us in our times of communion with him equips us to serve the needs of others as agents of the grace we have experienced in his presence.

There is tremendous power at work for our benefit in the practice of spiritual disciplines. We need to seek that power—the power of God's Word and Spirit—as it draws us into the presence of God's glory and shows us the wonders of his grace in new and more powerful ways. When we have met with the Lord Jesus in the practice of spiritual disciplines, we will be changed by his glory ever increasingly into his likeness. We will love him more and more, and we will go away from the disciplines of grace with a renewed resolve and greater power to serve him by loving others. This is what God has designed for us in our practice of the disciplines of grace. This is what we should seek above all else, and what we may reasonably hope to see happen in our lives.

### Questions for Study or Discussion

1. How would you describe your understanding of the disciplines of grace at this time? What are they for? What should you expect from them? What attitudes should characterize your use of these gracious tools?

2. Describe your experience of using the disciplines of grace. What do you experience as you are involved in them? In what ways is your life affected?

3. How would you be able to know if you were encountering the glory

of God on a regular basis in your practice of spiritual disciplines? Is this your normal experience? What keeps us from seeing the glory of God at these times?

4. Do you ever find in your practice of spiritual disciplines that you are settling for any of the lesser objectives discussed in this chapter (disciplines as an end in themselves, mere knowledge, disciplines for others' sake)? How might you be able to tell when this is becoming so in your spiritual exercises?

5. Take a moment and reflect on your practice of the spiritual disciplines in the light of this chapter. In what specific ways would you like to see improvement? How might you do so? Who are some people who could help you—through prayer, encouragement and accountability—to begin realizing more of the power of God in your practice of the disciplines of grace?

# 3

# tHe DISCIPLINes of GRace

*The secret of the easy yoke, then, is to learn from Christ how to live our total lives, how to invest all our time and our energies of mind and body as he did. We must learn how to follow his preparations, the disciplines for life in God's rule that enabled him to receive his Father's constant and effective support while doing his will.*
DALLAS WILLARD

*As for me, I will call upon God; and the LORD shall save me. Evening, and morning, and at noon, will I pray, and cry aloud: and he shall hear my voice.*
PSALM 55:16-17

*P*roper use of the disciplines of grace does not guarantee a life without trials, difficulties or sin. We are going to know defeat in the face of temptation, disappointment at the hand of loved ones and discouragement in our undertakings for the Lord. We will experience loneliness, sorrow, fear and doubt. We may even despair at times of being fruitful followers of Christ.

Nevertheless, through all these difficulties and more we may expect to grow in the grace and knowledge of the Lord as we persevere in the disciplines of grace, seeking the face of the Lord and drawing on his power to sustain and strengthen us for our daily walk with him. Hard times will come, as even our Lord Jesus promised (Jn 16:33). Yet his renewing and revitalizing grace is ever at hand, and the disciplines of grace are the place to turn, both for growing in the Lord and for dealing with the difficulties and trials of life.

It is not my purpose in this book to give an exhaustive and detailed description of the various spiritual disciplines that God has provided for our growth in him. Others have done that sufficiently well already.[1] Rather, I propose to give simply and briefly an overview of those disciplines that seem most prominent in Scripture in order to offer a convenient catalog for readers interested in assessing their own practice of the disciplines of grace and to present some guidelines for renewal through those disciplines.[2]

Only by understanding the nature and scope of the disciplines of grace can we use them as God intends. He has designed these special arenas of grace to draw us into an encounter with his glory so that by the power of his Word and Spirit we may be transformed increasingly into the image of Jesus Christ. Let's look at the various disciplines of grace in order to understand their role in helping us to grow in the grace and knowledge of the Lord.

### The Discipline of the Word of God

Foundational to all the disciplines of grace is intensive, personal time invested in the Scriptures, which are the Word of God written. Here I do not mean the kind of intensive study of Scripture that goes into preparation for preaching or teaching. Rather, my concern is with what may be called our *devotional* use of the Bible, that daily feasting on the Word that is so essential to growth in the Lord. Three practices in particular should be a part of our spiritual discipline.

*Reading the Word of God.* This special arena of grace will find us reading the Scriptures carefully, reflectively and comprehensively. Our tendency can be to limit ourselves to familiar parts of God's Word, reading them over and over because we have found them to be so helpful in the past. But careful and reflective reading of Scripture should be directed to all the counsel of God in both the Old and New Testaments. Since we believe that all Scripture is the inspired Word of God (2 Tim 3:15-17), every believer should follow some approach to Scripture reading that takes him or her through the entire Bible on a regular basis. The Scripture Union daily devotional guides, for example, provide both a schedule for reading the Bible through in one year and a study of the Scripture that covers the Old Testament once and the New Testament twice every

six years.[3] Various reading guides are available—such as McCheyne's—
which also take us through the entire Bible on a regular basis. Our
understanding of God's will can only be partial and dangerously incomplete without a commitment to constant reading and rereading of both
the Old and New Testaments, drawing from the treasury of both for our
spiritual enrichment (Mt 13:52).

*Study of God's Word.* Further, our time in the Word of God should
involve deep and careful study, during which we seek to attain a more
thorough understanding of a passage in the context of its book, the
author's corpus, its literary genre, and its purpose and place in the
unfolding progress of God's redemptive plan. This kind of study takes
time and is often most fruitfully carried out in a partnership with others.
Without such study our time in the Word of God will be shallow and can
become stale and unproductive. We can become easily convinced that we
have plumbed the depths of any passage when, in fact, we have only
barely skimmed the surface.[4]

Again, I do not have in mind here the kind of detailed exegesis
required for preparation to preach or teach. Rather, I want to urge those
for whom daily reading is an established practice a deeper examination
and analysis of the text to help them get beyond mere reading to a more
careful consideration both of the meaning of a passage of Scripture and
its applications to their own lives. In my own reading and study of Scripture, for example, I may read as many as three chapters—from both Testaments—as part of my devotions. At the same time, I am looking for a
few verses within that reading that I can pause over, consider more
deeply and seek to plumb for some daily application. These verses will
become the subject of my spiritual journaling, as I respond in writing to
what the text seems to require of me.

*Meditation and memorization.* The discipline of the Word of God should
also find us involved in meditation on and memorization of Scripture.
Each of these can provide opportunity for a more intensive and personal
encounter with God during our period of devotions, as well as for ongoing interaction with him during the course of the day. There are many
different ways to approach meditating on and memorizing God's Word,
and our practice of the discipline of God's Word will be incomplete without them.

Meditation should be part of our daily reading of Scripture. By focusing on the context of a passage, thinking about the key words and ideas, and asking questions about their meaning and significance, we can go deeper within a text than mere reading will allow. Let the words of the text suggest related passages, personal situations and needs, and opportunities for ministry. Pray through them until you see what they require of you or what the Lord is promising you in them. During the course of the day take a few moments to recall the passage and to reflect on it all over again, if only for a few moments. This will help you treasure the Word of God in your heart (Ps 119:11; Col 3:16). Meditation is a part of the study of God's Word and should help us reach some clear and concise conclusions about the meaning of Scripture for our lives.

I have always found memorizing Scripture to be tedious and difficult. Many people like to write favorite verses on cards and carry them around, reviewing them throughout the day until they have learned them by heart. Others will use a tool like the Topical Memory System of the Navigators ministry. My own practice has been to read, reread and meditate on a text until I become familiar with its contents, then to memorize it in my own words, so that I have the gist and substance of it, even though I may not have any particular version of the passage (NIV, KJV, etc.) word for word.

### The Discipline of Prayer

Prayer is perhaps the most distinctive of all Christian activities. Having been brought into eternal union with the Creator and sovereign Lord of the whole universe, in a relationship of child to Father, it is the most natural thing for us to talk with him often and about many different matters. In fact, so characteristic should prayer be in the life of a believer that we are expected to "pray without ceasing" (1 Thess 5:17), that is, to conduct our lives in an envelope of prayer, where conversation with our heavenly Father is a constant privilege and delight.

At the same time, prayer is for many believers the most difficult of disciplines. Abba Agathon, one of the desert fathers of the early church, tells us why:

> For every time a man wants to pray, his enemies, the demons, want to prevent him, for they know that it is only by turning him from prayer that they can hinder his journey. Whatever good work a man undertakes, if he perseveres in it, he will attain rest. But prayer is a warfare to the last breath.[5]

C. S. Lewis captured this same thought in a lighter, albeit equally serious vein when he had the demon adviser Screwtape counseling Wormwood concerning the matter of prayer: "The best thing, when it is possible, is to keep the patient from the serious intention of praying altogether."[6]

*Conversation with God.* Prayer is talking with God about things that are on our heart, offering praise and thanks to him for his goodness and grace, and interceding with him for the needs of others. In prayer we are involved in a dialogue with God. Thus we should leave time in prayer for *listening* to him—sensing the prompting of his Spirit as he guides us in prayer, enjoying the assurance of knowing that our prayers are heard and experiencing affirmation that he will answer our prayers according to his riches in glory in Christ Jesus. We can expect that prayer will be a struggle; our spiritual opponents will be ever at work trying to distract and discourage us. But God has promised to help us in our prayers so that we can know the joy and power that come from this important discipline (Rom 8:26).

*God's help in prayer.* Prayer is the most central of all the disciplines of grace, for it is part of every one of the rest of them. We practice this discipline of prayer in all the spiritual disciplines, as well as in a wide range of other activities. There may well be set times during the day that we devote to prayer such as in the morning, at meals and before retiring at night. It will help us during such times of prayer to remember that we do not know how to pray as we should (Rom 8:26). We are neither wise enough, strong enough, nor holy enough to bring to God in prayer all the matters and concerns that he desires to hear from us. So we need help. God promises that his Spirit will intercede for us when words fail or we are stumbling and bumbling our way along in a barely coherent manner. So we should not be frustrated or self-critical when words fail us in prayer or when we feel as though the words we're using are inadequate. Rather, we may rest in the provision of God's Spirit to make known to our heavenly Father the intentions and desires of our hearts in words far deeper and more significant than we could ever express.

But the Spirit can also use such aids as prayer guides, prayer lists, prayer formulas and prayer partners to help us gain the most from this discipline. There are even helpful books such as *The Book of Common Prayer* that can guide us in this important exercise.[7] In my own experience I have found using the psalms as the basis for my prayers to be the most satisfying and rewarding approach to prayer I have ever undertaken. Not only do I have the assurance of praying in words that are acceptable to the Lord, but I know that as I pray through the psalms, I am covering the subjects that he considers important for prayer. Whatever approach we take to prayer, we should see to it that we have as much help as we need so that our practice of this discipline will be full and rich, and so that we might gain the most benefit from our practice of prayer.

### The Discipline of Public Worship

Public worship provides an especially focused time for the practice of spiritual disciplines since it incorporates many of the various disciplines of grace into one compressed space of time. Prayer, silence, giving, and the reading and hearing of the Word of God are all brought to bear on our walk with the Lord during services of public worship. In addition, public worship is the setting within which we enter into the sacraments of grace, by which the Lord's mercy is dramatized to us, his presence is heightened among us, and we testify of our faith in him and seek renewal in his grace. Thus, our corporate worship of the Lord would seem to hold many opportunities for intensive, personal encounter with him each week.

However, like so many of the disciplines of grace, the practice of public worship can become a mere routine we observe on the Lord's Day as part of our cultural identity with the church. With little understanding of the role of or reason for the various elements of worship—the call to worship, hymns of praise and thanksgiving, confession of sin, giving, prayers and responses—it is easy to regard such elements as little more than preliminaries or anticlimaxes to the "real deal," which is preaching. In addition, among many congregations the elements that God has prescribed for his worship are in danger of being compromised or omitted altogether in order to make for a service of worship that will not offend unbelievers who may be visiting but that, indeed, will seem rather like home to them. This is done to encourage unchurched people to return again and again, but in the process it may compromise certain key aspects of the discipline of worship.

The worship wars erupting in so many congregations bear testimony to two critical issues: (1) the importance of worship in the life of faith and (2) our confusion as to the purposes, content and forms of worship. Some of this is healthy and will leave the church stronger in the next generation. Some of it, however, threatens to make a shambles of one of the disciplines of grace that God has provided for us to know him better and love him more and to go forth loving our neighbors as ourselves.

*Understanding the purpose of worship.* The place to begin in recovering a richer experience of worship is in understanding the purpose of this corporate discipline. We assemble on the Lord's Day to give praise and thanks to God, to offer ourselves anew to him and to hear his Word as it guides, comforts and encourages us. We should come to worship not seeking to gain something for ourselves—from the music, fellowship or preaching—but to give to God that of which he alone is worthy: our adoration, thanks, praise and heartfelt commitment. Worship is work—as we prepare for worship, enter into it, concentrate on it and devote our hearts to it—but we will find the work of worship to be exhilarating and exciting as we pour ourselves out in devotion and attention to God.

*Understanding the elements of worship.* Understanding worship also requires that we be clear about the various elements of worship—what they are and how we are to use them in worshiping the Lord. Why do we sing to the Lord, and how can we enter into singing with real awareness and conviction? What kinds of prayer are appropriate to public worship, and how may we participate in those prayers in a meaningful way? Is there some reason why we do things in the order we do in worship? How does preaching relate to all the other elements of worship? How do the sacraments fit into corporate worship? What are they for? How should we prepare for them? These are the kinds of questions we need to ask about the elements of public worship if we are going to be able to make the most of this special arena of grace that God has provided for us.[8]

## The Discipline of Observing the Lord's Day

I realize that observing the Lord's Day—sabbath keeping, as it is called—is a matter of controversy among some believers, both regarding which day is to be kept as well as whether or not keeping it is required of us at all. Here I shall assume that most readers accept the position that Sunday is the Lord's Day—changed from Saturday in the Old Testament to honor the day of Christ's resurrection and of God's resting from his work of redemption. Some argue that because sabbath keeping is not among the commandments of God that are repeated in the New Testament, it is no longer valid, and we need not concern ourselves with this discipline.

*Sabbath keeping a continuing discipline.* However, it could also be argued that observing the Lord's Day was an assumption and practice so deeply imbedded in the consciousness of those first believers that its repetition in the New Testament was considered unnecessary. The New Testament says little about a great many issues that contemporary Christians consider to be of great importance—such as singing in public worship. However, we recognize these as being so much a part of the life of the community of faith throughout Scripture that we faithfully carry the practice on in spite of the dearth of comment or instruction on it in the New Testament.

Further, it may be argued that the repetition of the commandment to observe the sabbath as one of the Ten Commandments is rendered unnecessary by virtue of its being a discipline established by God long before Moses met with him on Mt. Sinai, indeed, from the earliest days of creation (Gen 2:1-3). What God established as integral to the warp and woof of his good and perfect plan for his creation hardly needs mentioning with the Sinaitic legislation, as though it only had its origins there.

Throughout church history there has been little debate on this subject. The vast majority of theologians, commentators and pastors are in agreement that God has set aside one day in seven for himself, and that he intends for his people to observe that day by resting from their worldly vocations and avocations, and drawing close to him for spiritual rest and refreshment. The Lord's Day should thus be part of our practice of the spiritual disciplines as well.

*Some guidelines for observing the Lord's Day.* In addition to our participation in public worship (Heb 10:25), the Lord's Day provides an excellent opportunity for other activities that enable us to rest in him and be renewed for the week to come. These activities might include family prayer or worship, individual review and planning for the week ahead, reading Christian literature, spending time among the beauties of the creation and resting our bodies. If we fill the Lord's Day with worldly activities—shopping, sports and so forth—it will be difficult for us to muster the concentration on the Lord that resting in him requires. Therefore, we will need to plan our Lord's Day activities and stick to our plan if we are to gain the benefit from this weekly discipline that God intends.

## The Discipline of Giving

Giving is another controversial subject among Christians. Disagreement exists over whether tithing is still a valid practice, whether storehouse tithing is the biblical norm and whether pledging and faith promising are legitimate approaches to church and ministry budgeting.

*The practice of giving.* Nevertheless, some practice of giving—of our financial resources as well as our possessions and time—is a consistent feature of both Old and New Testament religion. Christians are expected to give liberally and gladly (2 Cor 9:7). Through various kinds of giving—of money, goods, services and the exercise of hospitality—we acknowledge God's ownership of all that we are and have, demonstrate the oneness of the body of Christ in its care for needy members, show that we understand the importance of the work of God's kingdom, help to relieve the needy in our community and around the world, and keep our natural covetousness and selfishness somewhat in check (Acts 4:32-37; 6.1-7; Rom 15:16-17).

*The value of giving.* Giving of our financial resources, possessions and time requires self-denial and can involve us in sacrifice—giving up cherished items and opportunities, and even daily necessities—in order to meet the needs of others. But it is in such giving that we, denying ourselves, encounter the Lord in his glory, learn to trust him more, find our hearts more compassionate toward those in need and grow in his grace. Thus our practice of the spiritual disciplines should involve some plan and practice of giving that will allow us to encounter the Lord as we do so in an intensive and personal way.

## The Discipline of Fasting

Jesus assumed that his followers would fast (Mt 6:16; 9:14). Saints in both the Old and New Testaments knew the value of this discipline in demonstrating repentance for sin, preparing for significant ministry, interceding for others and learning to depend more fully on the Lord. I suspect that most Christians today do not fast—at least not as a regular exercise of the disciplines of grace (although, given the conditions that Jesus imposed for fasting, that might be difficult to ascertain, see Mt

6:16-18). Fasting tends to be regarded as a discipline reserved for the super spiritual, or for extraordinary seasons of prayer and, from my observation, is not practiced as part of the disciplines of growth by many church members. Because this particular discipline is so routinely ignored on the part of Christians, and because fasting holds such potential for our growth in the Lord, I shall reserve more in-depth comments on it for a later chapter.

### The Discipline of Solitude

Many of the great saints of God in Scripture spent extended time alone with him, time to reflect on his work in their lives, recall his promises, seek his help, rest in him, meditate on his goodness or prepare for some significant new undertaking in his name. Seasons of solitude by such men as Moses, Elijah and the Lord Jesus were generally filled up with some discipline of the Word, prayer, fasting or meditation on the revelation of God's glory in the natural world. Like public worship, solitude provides a setting in which to bring the disciplines of grace together in a focused way for a compressed period of time, and it holds the potential of helping us to derive more benefit from these as a result.

The discipline of solitude takes time and requires us to retreat to some setting where we can be entirely separate from daily distractions, other human contact and the press of the world for an extended period of time, anywhere from an hour or two to a day or more. Immediately we are led to ask, "Where can I find the time for such activity?" I shall have more to say about this later. For now, let us settle in our minds that finding extended time alone with the Lord on some kind of regular basis is sufficiently important to our growth in the Lord that we must resolve that it will be part of our practice of the disciplines of grace.

### The Discipline of Silence Before the Lord

The final discipline I want to mention finds its expression within all the other disciplines of grace. We tend to treat our involvement in spiritual disciplines in a very active manner: praying without ceasing, reading and studying straight through to the end of our lesson or reading schedule, and worshiping the Lord from one element of worship to the next without pausing for any time to reflect or to listen to the Lord.

I once preached in the church of one of my students at Chesapeake

Theological Seminary. I would describe the worship style as contemporary and charismatic. We were led by a worship team and band who moved us from one song or prayer or testimony to the next without interruption and with a continuo of soft music as a bridge to whatever we did next. For over an hour we worshiped the Lord joyously and sincerely, taking time to confess our sins, to seek the blessing of his hand and to give our gifts to him before preparing our hearts for the ministry of the Word. From the opening of the service to the time I stood up to preach, music or speaking continuously filled the air in the worship center, with music continuing even under the prayers.

At the end of the service my student asked me how I would compare their worship with what I was familiar with in my Presbyterian tradition. I acknowledged that we had much in common, since the worship in his church employed all the elements of biblical worship, and in a reasonable and effective order. The forms in which they applied those elements differed markedly from my own experience, but I found that neither distracting nor a compromise with the biblical pattern of sound worship. What I did miss, I told my student, were any seasons of silence during the worship—any times to reflect on what we have just prayed or sung, to prepare for what we will be doing next, or just to listen for the Lord to speak to us from some testimony, hymn or message from his Word.

So also our practice of the disciplines of grace should include seasons of silence, of waiting on the Lord to prompt us by his Spirit, to bring to mind some sin in our life or some need of a brother or sister, to open up his truth to us in deeper and more relevant ways or to discover his will for some matter or other. Such seasons of silence give the Spirit of God opportunity to work on our hearts in ways specific to our needs, ways that he is not likely to employ when we are the only active participants in the disciplines of grace. By including times of silence in our practice of spiritual disciplines, we make them more of a dialogue between us and the Lord in which we are more likely to experience that intensive and personal encounter with him that our practice of the disciplines should provide.

### Recovering the Practice of Spiritual Disciplines
In the chapters that follow I shall suggest ways you might recover the practice of spiritual disciplines, rescuing some from being mere routines,

adding others and allowing them all to have more of their life-transforming effect in your life. The recommendations that follow come from my own experience and the testimony of others. I have found them to be effective in returning the practice of spiritual disciplines to my life whenever I have come to believe that those disciplines have slipped and become little more than spiritual routines. By spending more time in the disciplines of grace, intensifying the time I spend in them, adding new disciplines to my schedule and enlisting the help of others in my practice of spiritual disciplines, I have been able more and more to know the power of God's Spirit and Word at work in my life in the practice of spiritual disciplines. And while the transformation I seek is often slow in coming, I have the assurance that, indeed, God is at work in me, using the disciplines of grace to make me more and more the man he wants me to be in Christ Jesus.

Half the adventure of growing in grace is meeting with the Lord in the practice of spiritual disciplines. The other half is waiting on him to work out in us what he has shown us in those special arenas of grace, enabling us to grow in love for him and for our neighbors as ourselves. This is not something that mere involvement in spiritual disciplines will achieve; nor can we attain it through a firmer resolve or greater exertion of our own efforts. God gives spiritual growth as he works within us to will and do according to his good pleasure (1 Cor 3:7; Phil 2:12-13). He will bring growth in his way and time. However, we must apply ourselves earnestly and effectively to the means he has provided for growing in grace. And he has been pleased to give us the disciplines of grace as arenas in which we may expect to meet him face to face, to encounter his glory and to know the life-transforming power of his Spirit in intensely personal ways. As we enter faithfully into the practice of spiritual disciplines, looking to the Lord and waiting on him to work in us, we may expect to discover and experience more of their power to help us to grow in love for him and for others.

### Questions for Study or Discussion

1. Which of the disciplines of grace mentioned in this chapter do you practice as part of your own growth in grace? Which of those do you find to be most helpful? In what ways?

2. As you consider the whole range of spiritual disciplines that are

available to help us grow in grace, what concerns do you have about trying to improve your practice of the disciplines of grace or to add new ones to your schedule?

3. Review each of the disciplines introduced in this chapter. Of those you are not currently practicing on a regular basis, how can you see that they might help you to grow in the Lord?

4. Sometimes having a prayer partner or a person to encourage you in the practice of spiritual disciplines can be a great help. Can you think of someone who might help you? Are you part of any groups that could serve this purpose? How would you go about approaching such people to help you improve your practice of the disciplines of grace?

5. From what you have read so far in this book, how has your understanding of the nature, purpose and importance of spiritual disciplines grown? Have you seen any improvement in your own practice of the disciplines of grace? In what ways?

# 4

# tHe goaL of spiRituaL
# DISCIpLiNes

*Thousands are congratulating themselves, and even blessing God that they are
devout worshippers, when at the same time they are living in an unregenerate
Christless state, having the form of godliness, but denying the power thereof.
He who presides over a system which aims at nothing higher than formalism,
is far more a servant of the devil than a minister of God.*
CHARLES SPURGEON

*Now the end of the commandment is charity out of a pure heart, and of
good conscience, and of faith unfeigned.*
1 TIMOTHY 1:5

*F*or many of us, what Charles Spurgeon warned aspiring ministers of may be true for our practice of the disciplines of grace. We have
become satisfied with mere formalism, with going through the motions of
spiritual disciplines without realizing any of the purpose for which God
intended them. Should we be interrupted in the midst of our morning
devotions by someone asking what we're doing, we might reply, "I'm
having my devotions, can't you see?" In our minds having devotions—or
praying or going to church—is an end in itself, something we do because
we should, but which, in fact, results in very little evidence of a transformed life.

The first of the great desert fathers, Abba Anthony, said, "Whoever hammers a lump of iron, first decides what he is going to make of it, a scythe, a sword, or an axe. Even so we ought to make up our minds what kind of virtue we want to forge or we labour in vain."[1] Or as the old saying has it, aim at nothing and you'll hit it every time. For our purposes his advice is clear: our use of the disciplines of grace must be purposeful, according to the end for which God has given us these special arenas of grace. And that is that we might grow in grace and in the knowledge of our Lord Jesus Christ, being transformed from one encounter of God's glory unto the next, growing more and more into the very image of the Lord himself, according to our own needs and the opportunities for serving the Lord that he brings to us each day. Paul says we are to discipline ourselves for the purpose of godliness (1 Tim 4:7). Jonathan Edwards put it this way:

> We ought to be continually growing in holiness; and in that respect coming nearer and nearer to heaven. We should be endeavouring to come nearer to heaven, in being more heavenly; becoming more and more like the inhabitants of heaven, in respect of holiness and conformity to God; the knowledge of God and Christ; in clear views of the glory of God, the beauty of Christ, and the excellency of divine things, as we come nearer to the beatific vision. We should labour to be continually growing in divine love—that this may be an increasing flame in our hearts, till they ascend wholly in this flame—in obedience and heavenly conversation; that we may do the will of God on earth as the angels do in heaven; in comfort and spiritual joy; in sensible communion with God, and Jesus Christ.[2]

Augustine also weighed in on this matter, saying that we cannot truly come into the presence of God, into those arenas where his Word and Spirit are manifesting his divine glory and power, without growth in the Lord resulting. The "very vision of God, which is the end of looking," wrote the great African bishop, "has nothing further to which it can turn itself: and this is the truly perfect virtue, Virtue arriving at its end, which is followed by the life of blessedness. . . . For when the soul has once seen that unique and unfalsified Beauty, she will love it more, and unless she shall with great love have fastened her gaze thereon, nor any way declined from the view, she will not be able to abide in that most blessed vision."[3]

The purpose of spiritual disciplines is Christian growth, and if we are not growing—if we are continuing to struggle with the same sins, to be complacent about our mission in the Lord or to prefer the comforts and diversions of the world over the presence of God—then we need to realize that whatever spiritual disciplines we are employing have become little more than spiritual routines. And since they are not helping us grow, we need to consider ways of revitalizing those disciplines so that they might serve the purposes for which God intends them.

Of all the things that we might do to reclaim our practice of spiritual disciplines from the rut of routine, none is more important than recovering our understanding of the purpose of these disciplines and redoubling our efforts to focus our use of them on specific areas of needed growth and ministry opportunity in our own lives. The Holy Spirit is the author of Christian growth, and he will work much more effectively in those who are focused with him on that goal as they enter into the practice of the disciplines of grace.

### The Twofold Goal

What Paul wrote concerning the end of the commandment, or the goal of our instruction, is true of our practice of all the disciplines of grace: we are to grow in love for God and our neighbors. On these two objectives all our practice of spiritual disciplines must be focused. These are the great commandments, according to Jesus (Mt 22:36-40). It stands to reason that the disciplines of grace would be given in order to help us to carry out these most important instructions from the Lord. We must set our hearts during the practice of spiritual disciplines to grow in love for God and for our neighbors as ourselves, working diligently to overcome every obstacle that hinders growth, and seeking grace to advance in strength and wisdom for the service of God.

But what is it to love God? Or to love our neighbors? From where does such love come to sinful and selfish people such as we? And how can we enter the practice of spiritual disciplines so as to ensure that love will actually result from the time we invest there?

### Loving God

We must begin with learning to love God, for from our love for God flows all other love and all the fruit of Christian growth. Love for God is the motive for loving others. It provides the grace and strength we need to stay the course in the practice of spiritual disciplines and the walk of faith. Without a deep and growing love for God, everything else in the Christian life becomes mere formalism.

*Loving God is knowing him.* Loving God is, in the first place, knowing him as he is and not just as we would like him to be (Ps 91:14). How easy it is for us to acquire an understanding of God that is little more than a projection of our own minds concerning how we would like to think of him: God as our Father, our Friend and Companion, the all-understanding and all-forgiving Judge, the ever-ready-to-comfort-and-console One. All of these are true about God. But they are not the whole truth of who he is.

Or we may commit the mistake of thinking that God is just like we are—that he winks at sin, that he doesn't spend much time in his own Word and doesn't take it seriously, that he regards it as OK for us to take advantage of others for our own benefit and so forth. Nothing could be further from the truth (Ps 50:16-21).

To love God—to reverse the phrasing of an oldies classic—is to know him, to gain an ever-increasing understanding of his character, person, majesty, environment, purposes, works and plans. He has given us the disciplines of grace as opportunities to enter more fully into the knowledge of his divine character and power, as he reveals himself in his Word, rehearses his mighty works, speaks to us in the still, small voice of his Spirit, recalls to us the redeeming work of our Lord Jesus Christ and listens to our intercessions concerning our needs and those of others. The first goal of spiritual disciplines is to broaden and deepen our knowledge of God and to help us in keeping him before our minds throughout the day. As Dallas Willard has written, "If anyone is to love God and have his or her life filled with that love, God *in his glorious reality* must be brought before the mind and kept there in such a way that the mind takes root and stays fixed there."[4]

This is what the disciplines of grace can do for us like nothing else in our experience. Our approach to each of the disciplines and learning to love God must therefore be primarily to know God as he makes himself known, to give ourselves heart, mind and strength to seeing him as he is and embracing him accordingly.

*Loving God is delighting in him.* To love God is thus to know him. But the demons know God, and yet they do not love him. Hence, love for God is more than merely knowing him. It is delighting in him, finding joy, excitement and complete contentment in his presence, being thrilled with the knowledge that the God of heaven and earth is pleased to entertain us in his presence, to hear our prayers and to shape and mold us heart, mind and strength into works of art pleasing to him (Ps 37:4; 63:1-4; 73:25-28; Eph 2:10).

We all have things in our lives in which we take great delight—favorite foods or activities, places and things, people and times. How we look forward to those precious delights! What joy and satisfaction we derive from them! And how reluctantly do we cease from them when once we have begun to enjoy them.

Can we say that this is true of our relationship with God? That we delight in him so much that we cannot wait to be with him, are constantly seeking to be before his face and will only with the greatest reluctance allow ourselves to be distracted and drawn away? That we prefer the presence and fellowship of the Lord to any and every earthly delight?

To love God is to delight in him like this, and the disciplines of grace are the special arenas that God has given us for nurturing this delight in him so that we may go forth more and more in the enjoyment of God in the whole of our lives.

*Loving God is seeking him.* "O God, thou *art* my God; early will I seek thee" (Ps 63:1). "Seek the LORD, and his strength: seek his face evermore" (Ps 105:4). This only makes sense. If we know God as he is truly, and if we delight above all else to be in his presence, we will invest a great deal of time and energy in seeking him.

First, we will seek more time with him. Knowing God and delighting in him, we will look for every available moment to be in his presence, to look into his face and listen to the sweet words of his mouth. We will linger there, drinking in all the wonder and glory of our time with him, savoring each moment as more precious than anything else in our lives. Those who are truly seeking the Lord will look for ways to increase the time they have with him, both in the practice of spiritual disciplines per se and in disciplining the routines of their lives throughout the day.

But, second, seeking the Lord involves going deeper with him, intensifying our time with him in order to gain a clearer vision of his heart and of how we may bring our own hearts more consistently into rhythm with his. The moment we begin to feel satisfied with the time we are spending with the Lord is the moment we need to look for ways to intensify that time. For the Lord is infinitely deeper, more wonderful, more marvelous and majestic, more mysterious and powerful than we can ever comprehend. There is always more to know of him and, thus, greater delight for us to enjoy in knowing him.

But we must seek him earnestly and continually. Casual, routine seeking is not enough if we are to love the Lord with all our heart, mind and strength. As we give ourselves to moving from routine to renewal in our practice of the disciplines of grace, seeking the Lord at ever-deeper levels, we will discover new depths of joy in the Lord and be exposed in new and more powerful ways to know his glorious, transforming power and grace.

*Loving God is serving him.* Loving God involves carefully and constantly ascribing to him the worth of which he alone is deserving and going forth as living sacrifices for his name. Serving God in worship involves specific and sincere expressions of recognition concerning who he is, as well as of the many good things he has done. Our worship will be filled with praises and thanks to God that are grounded in his character and works, as well as in the blessings we personally have experienced through his grace. Such worship will be highly informed, deeply heartfelt, open and sincere, private and public, and increasingly a way of life (Rom 12:1-2). Each of the disciplines of grace provides opportunity for us to worship God in Spirit and in truth. Yet we will only know such worship when we have learned to use our disciplines as precisely that, and not as mere formalistic exercises entered into out of some sense of duty or obligation.

Loving God involves serving him throughout the course of our lives as well. All the saints of God are to be equipped for ministry in his name (Eph 4:12), and the disciplines of grace are a primary arena where such equipping can occur. Knowing God, delighting in him, seeking and worshiping him, how could we not desire above all else that those around us should also experience his mercy, grace and power? We are the vessels of the Lord to bear that grace to them (2 Cor 4:7-15), so that, coming under the power of God's irresistible love, they may join us in knowing and delighting in him, and in offering thanks and praise to his great and holy name. In our practice of spiritual disciplines our minds should be enlightened and our hearts incited to specific works of ministry that we may perform, in the power of God's Spirit, for the people around us, thus turning on them the love we have for our Father and proving that love in work and word toward our neighbors.[5]

The first goal of the practice of spiritual disciplines is to grow in love for God, to know him truly, delight in him completely, seek him earnestly and serve him devotedly in worship and ministry to others. Our spiritual disciplines are mere routines if they are not helping us consistently to grow in this way.

### Loving Our Neighbors

As I have suggested, loving our neighbors is the natural outworking of our love for God, when our hearts, overflowing with his grace and filled with his Spirit, constrain us to reach out to them in ways that show the reality of God's love for them. To love our neighbors is to be agents of God's grace, bearers of the good news of his forgiveness and love, aides along the journey of life, sources of strength in their times of need and reminders of the constant presence of their caring, forbearing God.

*Loving others is knowing them.* According to Paul in 1 Corinthians 13:4-7, such love is an active love. It takes the initiative to get to know others, discern their needs, listen to their concerns and reach out in appropriate ways according to the opportunity of the moment. Just as we might like to have others continuously showing the love of God to us—being patient with our follies and foibles, kind in their every word and gesture, freeing us from any controlling effort on their part, forgiving, sympathetic, forbearing, hopeful and longsuffering—so we go forth from the presence of God and in the power of God to show such love to all around us (Mt 7:12). We do not wait to be invited to love others; rather, after the example of the Lord, we go seeking those in need of his love and making ourselves available as agents of God's grace to touch them with the warmth of his renewing mercy and power.

Only as we work hard at getting to know others will we be able to appreciate their uniqueness and beauty and to discover their needs and concerns.

*Loving others is delighting in them.* To show the love of God for others we must learn to enjoy being with them. This will be hard for us to do as long as we conceive of our relationships in terms of what we will get out of them rather than what we might put into them. Our enjoyment in relationships should come from seeing and accepting others as they are and looking for ways to show them the love of Christ. Consider the many ways that the apostle Paul spoke of his delight in those to whom he wrote: "I long to see you" (Rom 1:11); "I trust to tarry a while with you" (1 Cor 16:7); "I thank my God upon every remembrance of you, always in every prayer of mine for you all making request with joy, for your fellowship in the gospel from the first day until now" (Phil 1:3-5); "ye are our glory and joy" (1 Thess 2:20).

Delighting in people means caring so much about them that we long for them to grow in grace with us. The apostle John reminds us that such love is a holy love, that is, it acts in accord with the righteous requirements of God's law (1 Jn 5:1-3). Thus the love we bear for others, and the delight we take in them, while it will be patient, kind and forbearing, will not be unqualified in its tolerance. It is not loving to condone the sinful ways of others, though longsuffering and gentleness will certainly govern the manner in which we approach them as fellow sinners. It is not loving to join others in sin, even though refusing to do so may risk a breach in our friendship (1 Pet 4:3-4). It is not loving to fail to confront those who are in their sins, as Paul confronted Peter out of love for God and for him (Gal 2:11). Loving our neighbors and delighting in them requires a purity in our lives and our relationships with them that insists on such in them as well but that works through active love—with patience, kindness, forbearance and truth—to encourage and nurture the holiness that love requires.

*Loving others is seeking them.* If we truly love others, we will seek to be with them, making time in our busy schedules for getting to know them, deepening our delight in them and encouraging them in the Lord. Just as Jesus came to seek and to save the lost (Lk 19:10), so we need to seek others in order that we might show the love of God to them as Jesus does to us. We will make time for them, go out of our way to be with them, take the initiative in contacting them and allow them more and more to become part of our lives.

It is very easy to fill our days with a personal agenda that allows little time for others. However, as we get to know the people around us and begin to delight in them, we will find that we are more inclined to seek to be with them for the mutual encouragement and joy that such times can afford.

*Loving others is serving them.* Finally, loving others means looking for ways to serve them, whether by word or deed. To love another is to desire the very best for that person and do everything that you can as often as possible to bring that very best to pass. What could be more wonderful, more replete with hope and joy and peace, more fraught with purpose and power, than encouraging them in knowing, loving, delighting in and serving God? And this can only be realized through knowing Jesus Christ and growing in him.

Thus the love we show our neighbors as we seek to serve them, whether saved or lost, will constantly point them to Jesus, urging them to consider him, to seek and follow him, and to grow in the grace that he alone provides for a full and abundant life (Jn 10:10).

The love that we have known from God, and in which we are growing for God, brings forth a similar love for our neighbors so that they too might come to know the love of Christ that passes knowledge (Eph 3:19). Our spiritual disciplines are mere formalities, pointless routines, unless they are engendering such love for our neighbors in our minds, hearts and lives.

But how can such love for God and our neighbors be nurtured? To what must we be especially attentive to as we enter the practice of spiritual disciplines? Paul says that such love, such an "unhypocritical faith" (to transliterate the Greek), flows out of the confluence of two primary streams—a pure heart and a good conscience or, more literally, a clean heart and a good moral understanding. If we are to grow in love for God and our neighbors, which is the goal of spiritual disciplines, then we shall have to give diligence in seeing that our hearts and minds are wrought upon by the Spirit and Word of God so that they become increasingly transformed by his glory and grace.

### Disciplining the Heart

The heart, as I am using the term, is the seat of the affections. It is that part of our being that exercises a formative role in how we think and what we say and do. Even a cursory glance, for example, at the book of Proverbs will show this. There we find that the heart can devise wicked schemes (6:18), give rise to wisdom and understanding (10:8, 20), harbor perversity and deceit (12:8, 20), know heaviness, hope, laughter and sorrow (12:25; 13:12; 14:13), incite to righteousness (15:28), play a significant role in our planning (16:9), be a source of many devices and counsels (19:21; 20:5) and resonate with the heart of another (27:19).

*Heart,* as used here, refers to the innermost being of a person, to some aspect of the image of God in us that has a powerful role for good or evil in our lives. Jesus said that the things that are in our hearts and the affections that issue from them can corrupt our lives (Mt 15:18-19). Edwards, referring to the affections—the inclinations of the heart—wrote:

> These affections we see to be the springs that set men a-going, in all the affairs of life, and engage them in all their pursuits; these are the things that put men forward, and carry them along, in all their worldly business, and especially are men excited and animated by these in all affairs wherein they are earnestly engaged, and which they pursue with vigour. We see the world of mankind to be exceeding busy and active; and the affections of men are the springs of motion.[6]

This being so, it is necessary to "keep thy heart with all diligence; for out of it *are* the issues of life" (Prov 4:23). The spiritual disciplines have been provided as primary arenas in which the Spirit of God can tame our hearts and make them serve the purposes of loving the Lord and our neighbors.

The spiritual disciplines have been given to us as arenas in which this watching over our hearts—training them to love God and our neighbors—can be exercised with great care and effect, equipping and preparing us for continued vigilance throughout the rest of our lives. Three things are necessary for us to do this effectively.

*Know the condition of a healthy heart.* First, we need to know what constitutes the condition of a healthy heart. We need to make sure we understand what kinds of affections we should be nurturing in our hearts. Edwards says,

> The affections are of two sorts; they are those by which the soul is carried out to what is in view, cleaving to it, or seeking it, or those by which it is averse from it, and opposes it.
>
>    Of the former sort are love, desire, hope, joy, gratitude, complacence. Of the latter kind are hatred, fear, anger, grief, and such.[7]

Thus, it is not so easy to say, for example, that love is always a positive affection and hatred always a negative one. For to love sin and hate righteousness are both indications of affections misdirected.

Rather, disciplining the heart requires that we understand each of the affections—how they are experienced and expressed, and what the proper objects are that we must direct them toward. A healthy heart is one in which all the affections are being rightly understood and properly nurtured and focused on the objects of our experience in ways that are pleasing to God.

As we enter into the practice of spiritual disciplines, therefore, we need to be sensitive to what the Lord desires to teach us about the affections of the heart: what they are, how we may recognize them in ourselves and how they ought properly to be focused. We will listen carefully for what the Scriptures have to say about such things as attitudes, aspirations, hopes, desires, longings, things to be sought and to avoid, and motivations. And we will meditate intently, pray for wisdom, talk with soul friends and reflect in moments of solitude on such matters, laboring to make certain that our understanding of them is that which God intends in his Word. We will seek the constant presence and power of the Spirit of God to bring our affections into line with the Scriptures so that we may love truly, from the heart, as the occasion requires.

*Being honest about our own hearts.* Second, disciplining the heart requires that we be honest about the condition of our own hearts in relation to what the Scriptures teach about affections. We will never grow to love righteousness so long as our hearts continue to love sin. We will be hindered in hating sin so long as our hearts begrudge the time required in spiritual disciplines. Lingering doubts as to the reliability of God's Word will dampen hope, faith and obedience. Ingratitude quenches the Spirit of God. Only by identifying the presence of misunderstood or misdirected affections in our own hearts can we begin the hard work of clarifying and redirecting them for God's glory and our own growth in grace.

In the disciplines of grace we are invited to be completely honest before the Lord, who knows our hearts at any rate (Ps 90:8; Is 1:18-20). We may come before him without fear of condemnation and seek grace to help in our time of need (Rom 8:1; Heb 4:16). As the light of God's Word shines on our hearts, as we talk with him concerning the sin that remains in us and as we seek his guidance and presence for the whole of our lives, he will make plain to us the nature of our heart's health and show us specific areas of affections that need to be disciplined by his grace. As we learn to listen attentively and agreeably, we will be in a position to trust him to begin transforming the state of our hearts and the affections that issue from it according to the image of the Lord.

*Seeking the transforming grace of God.* Finally, disciplining the heart requires that we wrestle with the Lord until he blesses us in our hearts, putting in place the affections that he desires and directing them at the objects of our experience in ways pleasing to him. Here it should be clear why we need to make better use of our time for the study of Scripture, in prayer and meditation, solitude and silence, and all the other disciplines, drawing strength from the Lord in order to resist temptation, stand firm in the face of trials and seize the opportunities for ministry that he brings into our path. The richer the time we invest in disciplining our hearts, the greater the likelihood that they will, in fact, be disciplined, that is, that the proper affections will be in place and properly directed, when the need for them arises in our lives. Faced with temptation, trial or opportunities for service, we need our hearts to be strengthened and encouraged by the Lord if words and works pleasing to him are going to ensue (2 Thess 2:16-17). The more we work at training our hearts, submitting them to the power of God's Word and Spirit, the more we will be able to respond according to the will of God in the tight squeezes and open doors of our lives. And the more our disciplined hearts, moved by proper affections, lead us to Christlikeness in our everyday lives, the more such responses will become habitual, permanent parts of who we are in Christ. Which is to say, the more we live like Christ, the more we, in fact, become like him, transformed from glory to glory through the practice of spiritual disciplines, as our hearts grow in love for him and for our neighbors as ourselves.

### Disciplining the Mind

The sad state of the Christian mind has been lamented for nearly forty years now.[8] Contemporary believers do not regard the mind as much of an active player in the life of faith. We are more concerned with feelings, and those feelings—affections—are often poorly understood and woefully misguided. Yet, as Edwards observed, "Christians should not always remain babes, but should grow in Christian knowledge; and leaving the food of babes, they should learn to digest strong meat."[9] In other words, it is part of our calling to grow in grace that we should "gird up the loins of [our] mind" in the cause of Christ and his kingdom (1 Pet 1:13).

Edwards comments, "The faculty by which we are chiefly distinguished from the brutes, is the faculty of understanding. It follows then, that we should make it our chief business to improve this faculty, and should by no means prosecute it as a business by the bye."[10] We must not, in other words, take a merely casual "I'll get to it when I can" approach to growing in our minds. Rather, we must seek to discipline our minds as earnestly as we are seeking to discipline our hearts. For unless both are disciplined to serve the purposes of love, little in the way of an "unhypocritical faith," a faith that loves God and our neighbors, will be in evidence in our lives.

Edwards cites the advantages of disciplining our minds:

> Knowledge is pleasant and delightful to intelligent creatures, and above all, the knowledge of divine things; for in them are the most excellent truths, and the most beautiful and amiable objects held forth to view. . . . This knowledge is exceedingly *useful* in Christian practice. . . . The more you have of rational knowledge of divine things, the more opportunity there will be, when the Spirit shall be breathed into your heart, to see the excellency of these things, and to taste the sweetness of them. . . . Again, the more knowledge you have of divine things, the better will you know your duty; your knowledge will be of great use to direct you as to your duty in particular cases. You will also be the better furnished against the temptations of the devil.[11]

Disciplining our minds can be both a pleasurable and practical exercise, increasing our delight in the Lord and equipping us to love him and our neighbors more completely.

How, then, shall we discipline our minds to grow in grace?[12]

*Recognizing the presence of unbiblical ideas.* Paul's advice in Ephesians 4:17-24 is concise: we must put off our sinful nature, with its unbelieving and hardened mind, and be wholly renewed in Christ, beginning with our minds. First, recognize the presence of unbiblical ideas in your mind. To one degree or another the ideas, agendas and enticements of the unbelieving world influence us all. Advertising, pop culture, the demands of our work, our relationships with others, the whole ambiance of our postmodern society—all these expose us to views of life inconsistent with biblical teaching. Some of these we absorb without even thinking. We may profess to be born-again followers of Jesus Christ and devoted to his Word, but our minds are unknowingly clouded with the darkness of unbelief. This can be a major source of our inability to realize more of the fullness of life that Christ intends for us. Francis Schaeffer wrote:

> I am impressed by the number of times I am asked by Christians about the loss of reality in their Christian lives. Surely this is one of the greatest, and perhaps *the* greatest reason for a loss of reality: that while we say we believe one thing, we allow the spirit of the naturalism of the age to creep into our thinking, unrecognized.[13]

Only as we begin to recognize the presence of foreign elements in our outlook and thinking will we be able to challenge and eradicate them, replacing them with insights and understandings more in agreement with biblical truth.

Thus during our practice of the disciplines of grace we need to be asking God to search our hearts and minds, to show us any areas of our thinking—relative to work, family, relationships, avocations, finances and all the rest—that might still be shrouded in the darkness of unbelief (Ps 139:23-24). Let the light of God's Word and the penetrating power of his still, small voice challenge your thinking in every area of your life, so that you can see where unbiblical thinking and ideas are still lurking. Let the light of his eternal truth shine on the dull light of any worldly thinking you may still be harboring, and you will begin to see more clearly the excellency and beauty of his truth (Ps 36:9).

*Attacking unbiblical ideas.* Once unbiblical views have been identified, they need to be attacked with a view to laying them aside, supplanting them by biblical insights and understandings. Unbiblical ideas and thoughts inhabiting the conscious or subconscious regions of our minds will work to undermine our belief and trust in God. They must be eradicated, taken captive and made to serve the purposes of Christ (2 Cor 10:5).

This will require an all-out assault on the redoubts of unbelief yet lingering in our minds. We must know where such enemies have hidden themselves. Perhaps our view of money is based more on the practices of the world than on the teaching of God's Word, and as a result, we are robbing God and our neighbor by failing to use our wealth as God intends. Here we will need to study what the Scriptures teach about such matters as giving, the role of possessions, the use of money, the simple lifestyle, compassion and generosity, and so forth until biblical ideas begin to supplant the worldly thinking that is leading us to use our wealth in unbiblical ways. We will have to pray and fast for God to give us the wisdom and courage to make whatever changes will be needed in order to bring our financial practices more into line with the good and perfect will of God for our lives. We may need to consult with a soul friend in order to develop a workable plan and establish some meaningful accountability. In all these ways the disciplines of grace can serve to help us recognize and eradicate the mindset of unbelief and to be renewed in the mind of Christ.

*Being renewed in our minds.* Finally, we must work to wed our renewed minds to our renewed hearts so that we may go forth in joyful obedience to the Lord in the whole of life. At the same time that we are disciplining our minds for new thinking, we must be working to discipline our hearts so that we may truly be renewed in the spirit of our mind and go forth to put on the new person that we are becoming in Christ. We must set our affections on the things that we are learning about Christ's plan and rule, removing them from where they have been lodged, on earthly ideas and practices, and refocusing them on the new understandings we are gaining through our time in the disciplines of grace (Col 3:1-3). This will enable us to begin developing a new vision of ourselves as the servants of Christ, seeing our lives as they will be once our life has been disciplined along with our minds and hearts, and setting our hearts to desire that new vision and that new life above our former way of thinking and being.

The importance of the spiritual disciplines in this process should be obvious, especially of making sure that our disciplines are precisely that and not mere formalistic routines. For we will never grow in godliness or achieve a disciplined life of loving God and loving our neighbors if our involvement in the disciplines of grace is less than what God intends for us. A more careful focusing of our use of these disciplines can help to ensure that they will serve to reveal the glory of God to us and transform us increasingly into the very image of Jesus Christ.

### Questions for Study or Discussion

1. How would you describe the focus of your spiritual disciplines at this time? Can you see any ways this might be improved?

2. Reflect on this chapter's teaching about loving God and others.

How well does this describe your own love? Where do you need to grow?

3. How well do you understand the nature and role of affections? How can you begin to concentrate more on these in your practice of spiritual disciplines?

4. How can repentance and faithful obedience begin to be more consistently in evidence in your life?

5. In what ways can you see that your practice of the disciplines of grace can help you to grow in love for God and your neighbor?

# 5

# preparing for renewal
# in prayer

*Personally it is our repeated experience that in the depths of our hearts, at the
point where we disclose ourselves to the Eternal One, all the rays of our life
converge as in one focus, and there alone regain that harmony which we so often
and so painfully lose in the stress of daily duty. In prayer lies not only our unity
with God, but also the unity of our personal life. Movements in history, therefore,
which do not spring from this deepest source are always partial and transient, and
only those historical acts which arose from these lowest depths of man's personal
existence embrace the whole of life and possess the required permanence.*
ABRAHAM KUYPER

*And all things, whatsoever ye shall ask in prayer, believing, ye shall receive.*
MATTHEW 21:22

*B*efore discussing ways of improving your practice of the spiritual disciplines, I need to emphasize something that was mentioned in a previous chapter. That is that spiritual growth is the Lord's work. Only he can show us his glory in life-changing ways. God alone is able to revitalize our practice of the disciplines of grace and bring renewal to our lives. Certainly we must be willing to "work out [our] salvation" (Phil 2:12) by submitting with greater care and devotion to the disciplines of grace he has provided for us. But unless we are waiting on the Lord, looking to him and constantly seeking his strength and glory, we will never realize any improvement in our spiritual lives, no matter how many or varied our disciplines may be.

And the place to begin seeking him and the renewal he can bring is in prayer.

Prayer provides a framework for the practice of all the disciplines of grace. Whether we are studying God's Word, fasting, worshiping together, retiring before him in silence and solitude, observing the Lord's Day or practicing the discipline of giving, without prayer our use of these disciplines will lack the power of God for transforming us increasingly into the very image of the Lord. Similarly, as prayer is the framework for all the disciplines, so also it must be the starting point for improving or increasing our practice of these means of growth.

The following chapters offer many suggestions about ways to improve your use of the disciplines of grace. In this chapter I argue for the importance of prayer as the starting point for beginning to seek renewal in the spiritual disciplines. Then I offer some suggestions concerning how you can wait on the Lord in prayer for his guidance and help as you consider the best course to follow in moving from routine to renewal in the practice of spiritual disciplines.

## The Role of Prayer in Preparing for Renewal

If we wish to experience the work of God in revitalizing our practice of the disciplines of grace, we need to prevail upon him in prayer, even as we prepare for whatever course of action we may choose. This is true for at least ten reasons.

*God commands us to pray.* We can hardly expect to have much of a meaningful relationship with God or encounter his glory in and benefit from the disciplines of grace if we fail to adhere to his most fundamental commands. If, for example, we refuse to call upon him in prayer as he requires:

> Offer unto God thanksgiving; and pay thy vows to the most High: and call upon me in the day of trouble: I will deliver thee, and thou shalt glorify me. (Ps 50:14-15)

> Call unto me, and I will answer thee, and shew thee great and mighty things, which thou knowest not. (Jer 33:3)

> Ask, and it shall be given you; seek, and ye shall find; knock and it shall be opened unto you. (Mt 7:7)

What could be clearer? God commands his people to pray. If we are slow to submit to this command to pray as we should, or if we rush ahead relying on our own strength for renewal, how can we expect to know the blessings he alone can give us? Many Christians wonder why their lives in Christ are so flat, unexciting and lacking in fulfillment. Look to their prayers. We may expect to find a direct correlation between the amount of time spent in prayer, the quality of those prayers, and the degree of satisfaction and power they know in their daily walk with Christ.

As we think about moving from routine to renewal in the practice of the disciplines of grace, we need to look to God for guidance, wisdom, strength and the grace that we need. By waiting in obedience on him in prayer, earnestly seeking him and openly confessing our need of him, we may expect to find his presence and power more readily available to us in the spiritual disciplines.

*Prayer reminds us of our need for God.* Augustine noted that people are prone to depend upon themselves, to live their lives in their own strength and according to their own ideas of what is right for them. He wrote, "This desire for sovereignty is a deadly corrosive to human spirits."[1] We want to do it on our own, find our own way, figure it out all by ourselves. But this insistence on running our own lives our own way on our own strength is a sad mistake and can leave us frustrated and disappointed, especially where spiritual disciplines are concerned.

However, when kneeling before the Lord, turning over to him all the matters that so befuddle and confuse us and that would defeat and destroy us, we are reminded that only he is strong enough to carry us through each day. We cast our burdens upon him in the confident belief that he will bear them for us (1 Pet 5:8). As we do, we not only tap into the rich wellspring of his everlasting love, but we steer away from the icebergs of self-reliance that can so easily rip open the hull of our ship of faith. The more we come to God, the less will be our propensity to depend upon our own wisdom, wile or will when push comes to shove in the hard places of life. This is as true of our use of the spiritual disciplines as it is of any other aspect of our lives. Because prayer keeps us mindful of our need to depend on the Lord and not ourselves, we ought to turn to it as the place to begin preparing for renewal in spiritual discipline.

*Prayer lets us be ourselves—safely.* Prayer is the only place I know where I can be completely myself—in all my wretchedness, filthiness, foolish-

ness and ignorance—and not be judged for it. There is no condemnation
for those who are in Christ Jesus (Rom 8:1), so when we come to our
heavenly Father in his name, he is not going to condemn us, no matter
how feeble or faltering our approach to him.

As we begin to seek renewal in our use of the disciplines of grace,
prayer provides a context in which we are free to bring forth the dirty
laundry of our most secret sins (Ps 90:8). Have we been lazy or negligent
in the disciplines? Are we easily distracted or quick to rush off to other
things? Are our attitudes not what they ought to be? In prayer we may
be honest about all these things as we ask the Lord to search us and show
us the ways that our practice of the disciplines of grace has been wanting
(Ps 139:23-24). By committing to a season of preparation in prayer, we
may openly and honestly allow the Lord to search us and bring to light
any obstacles to renewal that might be in our lives. Then we may cry out
to him to give us the strength to deal with these obstacles before we move
ahead in determining a course of renewal.

*Prayer is the way to blessing.* God invites us to seek from him the satisfaction of our every need (Jer 33:3). This is true of our need for spiritual
renewal just as it is for every other area of our lives. He knows exactly
what we need as we prepare to address our practice of the disciplines of
grace, even before we come to him (Mt 6:8); yet, he is not likely to satisfy
those needs apart from prayer (Jas 4:2).

Spiritual renewal through the practice of spiritual disciplines is the
way to know the blessings of God with greater consistency and power. It
makes sense, therefore, as we begin to consider ways of moving from
routine to renewal in the means of grace, to seek the Lord in prayer for
his blessing even in this area of our lives.

*Prayer maintains the devil's defeat.* As we have seen, the devil does not
want us to pray, much less to know the glory of God that leads to transformed lives. Yet the Lord Jesus Christ has thoroughly defeated the
devil and his fiendish allies (Mt 12:22-29; Col 2:8-15). Christ's perfect
righteousness and saving death avail for our shortcomings, and his resurrection from the dead is the proof that God receives him as our Justifier.
Even now he intercedes for us at the Father's right hand, making our
needs and requests known through his blood and righteousness (1 Jn
2:1-2). He has given us his Spirit to lead us into all truth, fill us with
life-changing power and bring forth fruit consistent with his character

(Jn 16:13; Acts 1:8; Gal 5:22-23). All this can only be realized by beginning in prayer. When we turn to prayer, we occupy ground the Lord has secured in his victory over the devil. Prayer is a powerful weapon in the arsenal of the Lord (Eph 6:10-20). It keeps us in touch with our commander in chief, focuses our attention on his glorious throne and victory, drowns out the distracting voice of our adversary and sends him on his way looking for someone else to devour (Jas 4:7; 1 Pet 5:8).

As we prepare for renewal in our use of the disciplines of grace, we can expect the devil to be hard at work to discourage and distract us. We may be tempted to think that we can't really know any improvement in this area. We may put off making improvements or increasing our use of the disciplines for one reason or another. A myriad of excuses for resorting to the status quo and simply trying harder will flood our minds. All of this is the devil seeking to keep us from the spiritual renewal God promises.

Through prayer we frustrate the devil's attempts to claim some victory in the midst of his defeat. Prayer enables us to maintain his humiliation as well as to further our own progress in the life of faith. As we begin to prepare for renewing our use of the disciplines of grace, it makes sense to embark upon a preliminary season of prayer to keep the devil in his place as we seek the renewing grace of the Lord.

*Prayer helps us get beyond the flesh.* Most of us do not live lives of high adventure and romance. We crawl out of bed in the morning, get ourselves ready for the day, head off to work or school, drag ourselves through our daily routines, come home, eat, read the papers or watch TV, and just barely make it to bed before we crash, exhausted. Life, in short, can be dull and routine at times—indeed, perhaps much of the time.

The same can be true of our use of the disciplines of grace.

Given this situation, we tend to harbor low expectations about what our lives might be like or what our times of devotion might actually yield. Most of us do not envision ourselves as great saints of the Lord, leading the charge for his army against the forces of darkness in the advancement of his kingdom. We don't expect to encounter the glory of God in the course of reading his Word or participating in public worship. We consider ourselves to be ordinary followers of the Lord who are merely trying to hold down our place in the Lord's tent, adhering to our spiritual routines and doing whatever comes our way as best we can, given the limitations of our flesh.

Too bad.

We serve a God who is able to do exceeding abundantly above all that we could ever think or ask (Eph 3:20). The problem for many of us is that we hardly ever think of ourselves as servants of such a God with unlimited potential to behold his glory and be used for his kingdom. And, since we hardly ever think such lofty thoughts, we don't bother to ask God to make them true for us.

It may be hard to imagine our practice of the disciplines of grace as being anything other than what we have always known them to be—fairly interesting but unexceptional routines. But, as we have seen, this does not fit with what God has planned for us in these special arenas of grace.

Prayer provides a context in which we can escape the limitations of our flesh as we prepare for spiritual renewal. In prayer our vision of God is enlarged. As our vision of God expands, our sense of what he is capable of doing in, through and with us grows as well. We become bolder, more confident in our approach to him, more willing to ask great things of him and more likely to believe that he will answer them. As we pray this way, we will see areas that we might improve or increase our practice of the disciplines of grace, trusting in his power to guide and help us. We will begin to believe that he can do it. He can enable us to make the sacrifices, find the time, take on new challenges and enter into his power in ways we never have before. Thus prayer can help us to get beyond the limitations of our flesh as we consider a course of action for moving from routine to renewal in our practice of the disciplines of grace.

*Prayer is transformational.* Consider just a few things that Scripture tells us are possible as a result of prayer: Our daily needs will be met through prayer (Mt 6:11; 7:8). We can know peace in the midst of trouble (Phil 4:6-7). We can move beyond guilt and shame to become powerful witnesses for the Lord (Ps 51:10-15). The eyes of our hearts can be opened so that we can understand more of God's Word and experience more of his power (Eph 1:15-19). We can live in a manner worthy of the Lord, be pleasing to him in all respects and bear much fruit for his glory (Col 1:9-10).

God, who can do such things in us through prayer, can renew our practice of the spiritual disciplines as well. As we address the question of how best to recover a right use of the disciplines of grace, we must prepare ourselves by concentrated, extended prayer for the transforming power of God in our lives.

*Prayer makes us more like Jesus.* It is the burden of God's Spirit, working in the disciplines of grace by means of the Word of God, to transform us increasingly into the very image of Jesus Christ our Lord (2 Cor 3:12-18). In this life we are to become more like him and less like ourselves, as John the Baptist observed: "He must increase, but I must decrease" (Jn 3:30). That Jesus was often given to prayer and spiritual disciplines is clear from the testimonies of the evangelists. The more we pray, the more we emulate the Lord and enter an arena where the work of God's Spirit can transform us into the very image of Jesus. If we want to be like Jesus in our public lives, caring for others, serving them, bearing witness to the kingdom of God—which are the fruit of spiritual disciplines—we shall have to work harder to become more like him in our private lives, as Dallas Willard argues throughout *The Spirit of the Disciplines.* And that means, in the first instance, more time in prayer.

Prayer was a powerful source of daily strength for the Lord. As we devote ourselves to prayer, both in preparing for renewal and in the practice of spiritual disciplines, we will bring ourselves heart, mind and strength into that posture that so characterized him. And we will find there both grace to help in our time of need and the power of God's Spirit at work conforming us more perfectly to the image of the Lord. In prayer he can show us how to proceed in recovering a right use of the disciplines of grace.

*Prayer keeps us in focus.* How easy it is to become distracted by all the mundane activities that characterize our lives. Every day, as we slog through our schedules and routines, the materialism, hedonism, sensuality and temporality of the world in which we live confront us. We could easily come to believe that this earthly life is what matters most and that we should devote the better part of our energies not to more involvement in spiritual disciplines but to getting the most out of this life while we can.

But Paul counsels us otherwise. He tells us to set our hearts and minds on the things of the Lord, to keep the vision of Christ exalted and enthroned before our eyes throughout the day, and to do all that we do in such a way as to represent him as ambassadors of his kingdom (1 Cor 10:31; 2 Cor 5:17-20; Col 3:1-3). This is the full and abundant life to which we have been called.

Prayer can be a great help to us in this calling, especially as we seek renewal in the disciplines of grace that are the training ground for such a life. Prayer keeps us focused on who we really are rather than who we might seem to be in the midst of a materialistic age. Commitment to prayer as a way of preparing for renewal in the disciplines of grace can help us to sort out our priorities in the light of our eternal callings as the sons and daughters of God, so that we are better able to seek first the kingdom of God and his righteousness, leaving everything else to him (Mt 6:33).

*Prayer engages us with God.* There is nothing quite like prayer to bring us fully into the presence of God, to enable us to know his power and glory and help in all their rich fullness. In prayer we enter the very throne room of the Father, by his invitation, for the purpose of bringing our requests to him and finding grace to help in our times of need (Heb 4:16). As we enter, the Son of God, our great High Priest, rises at the Father's right hand to welcome us and to advocate our needs to his Father and ours (Acts 7:55; Heb 4:14-15; 1 Jn 2:1). And when we speak, not knowing how to pray as we ought, the Spirit of God himself intercedes for us, using language appropriate to the setting and bearing our requests before the Lord in power (Rom 8:26-27). In no other aspect of the life of faith are we as consciously engaged with the persons of the Godhead as in prayer. What a rich privilege and great blessing for those who resort to it often!

Thus we may expect, as we prepare for renewing our practice of the disciplines of grace, that prayer will bring us before the Lord in all his glory so that he might counsel, strengthen and help us in this glorious challenge. By embarking on a season of preparation in prayer, we can have greater assurance that the course of action we choose as we move from routine to renewal will be just the one the Lord intends for us so that we might grow in grace and in the knowledge of our Lord and Savior.

### Preparing for Renewal in Prayer

There are as many ways to prepare for renewal in prayer as there will be readers of this book. My purpose in this section is not to prescribe a proven course of action that you can follow in prayer as you begin to seek the Lord for renewal in the practice of the disciplines of grace.

Instead I am suggesting some activities that serve as focal points for waiting on the Lord in prayer, looking to him to reveal the state of your spiritual disciplines and areas of needed improvement. Any or all of them can be of help as you move from routine to renewal in this most important area of your life.

*Take your time.* We tend to be impatient. We want to jump in and get right to work. But things worth doing are worth doing well, and this means we will need some time for reflection before we embark on a new course in the practice of spiritual disciplines. Like Nehemiah surveying the wall of Jerusalem (Neh 2), we need to know the specific nature of the damage before we adopt new remedies for our spiritual lives.

You should plan to take some time for this period of preparation. The worst thing you could do would be to rush into the following chapters, picking up and patching on every idea or suggestion you find there in order to bring new vitality to your practice of the disciplines of grace. That would be to proceed on your own strength rather than in the wisdom and power of God. Not all the recommendations that follow will fit your needs. Instead, as you continue working through this book, commit to a week or even a month of just waiting on the Lord in prayer, asking him to speak to you about your needs in this area, looking to him for new attitudes, objectives and priorities.

*Ask a friend to help.* There is wisdom in having a friend to pray with and for you as you begin this process of self-discovery and renewal. Find someone who cares about you, a person you can trust and who you know is faithful in prayer. Explain what you want to do and ask him or her to commit to praying with you during this period of preparation. Provide some specific requests: that you might better understand the disciplines of grace; that you might come to see areas of needed improvement in attitudes, goals and practice; that the Lord would help you with your priorities and show you a course of action for renewal.

Ask your friend to meet with you once or twice during the period you have set apart for preparation in prayer. Share what you have done and what you are discovering. Ask for feedback. Offer new requests and pray together. Having someone with you in this preparatory stage will make you more responsible in your preparation and your preparation more fruitful.

*Commit to prayer.* Above all, this should be a season of devoted prayer,

prayer focused on you and your practice of the disciplines of grace. You may add some of the suggestions that follow to your regular time of prayer, either in the morning or at night. Or you might try setting aside some time each day—say fifteen minutes or so—when you can concentrate on prayer for the renewal of your spiritual disciplines. However you approach this season of preparation, make prayer for renewal a daily undertaking, so that you are consistently focusing on the disciplines of grace and seeking the will of God for your life in them all. Now a few suggestions for your prayers.

First, you might find it helpful to take the questions for study or discussion from each of the first five chapters as the subject of your prayers, one section of questions per day. That will give you twenty-five days' worth of topics for your prayers. As you reflect on each question, ask the Lord to help you to be honest, to open your heart and mind to new insights and to speak to you clearly about his will for your life in the practice of spiritual disciplines.

Second, take a look at the other activities in your life to consider whether your priorities and time usage are what they ought to be. Spend some time before you retire each evening reviewing your day in prayer. You might use Ephesians 5:15-17 or Psalm 90:12 as scriptural focal points for your prayer. Ask the Lord to show you any areas of wasted time, wrong priorities in the use of your time or opportunities to bring the disciplines of grace into more of your time each day. If you did this for twenty-five days, while you were praying through the questions to these first five chapters, you could expect the Lord to show you areas where your use of time could be improved for the sake of spiritual disciplines.

Third, before your devotional reading each day pray one of the sections of Psalm 119. There are twenty-two of these, corresponding to the letters of the Hebrew alphabet.[2] As you pray each section, ask the Lord to speak to you about your attitudes toward spiritual discipline, the goals you have set for your walk with him and your actual practice of the disciplines of grace. Pay attention to the verbs in these sections. Look at the psalmist's declared intentions and desires. How does your own practice match up to these? Let the Lord speak to you through this psalm as you pray it reflectively, focusing on your practice of the disciplines of grace and any areas for needed renewal.

Fourth, review in prayer each of the spiritual disciplines introduced in chapter three. Take one a day, praying through it as often as necessary throughout your time of preparation. Ask the Lord to help you understand the nature and role of each of these disciplines and to show you specific ways you might hope to benefit. Review each one as often as you need to until he impresses its importance on you. Study the Scripture references provided for each one and ask the Lord to show you whether you are living in obedience to his good and perfect will in each case. Ask him to make clear whether your practice of any of the disciplines has become a mere routine and to guide your thinking as you consider how to recover a right use of the disciplines. Wait on him and persevere in prayer until he makes his will for you clear.

Fifth, in all your times of prayer remember to make renewal of the disciplines of grace a matter of concern. Let your Bible study group pray for you. Share with your family and friends, as well as your pastor and other church leaders. Before your meals, thank the Lord for this season of preparation and remind him that you are looking to him to reveal your needs and show you a course of action. Don't miss a single opportunity in prayer to make this request known. Ask, seek and knock, and you can expect that he will answer, reveal and open to you.

Finally, make some notes from each of your times of prayer and use them as a focus for prayer during each subsequent day. Carry them with you for review and additional prayer. Add to the notes each time you enter into prayer for your practice of the disciplines of grace. Ask the Lord to give you clear understanding and a firm resolve as he speaks to you about ways to move from routine to renewal in the practice of spiritual disciplines.

This time of preparation can be a valuable opportunity for focusing on your use of the disciplines of grace as you reflect on your current practice and seek the wisdom and power of God for renewal. Wait on him in faith, seeking insights from his Word and power from his Spirit to point you in the direction of renewal. Believe that he can speak to you, give you insight and wisdom, guide and direct you, and enable you to take whatever steps may be indicated. Remember that whatever you ask of him in prayer, believing, you will receive (Mt 21:22; Jas 1:5-7). Recovering a right use of the disciplines of grace can be a turning point in your history with the Lord. Let that turning point begin in prayer, and you can be assured that he will grant your requests and meet your needs according to his riches in glory by Christ Jesus (Phil 4:19).

### Questions for Study or Discussion

1. Do you believe that God is able to do exceeding abundantly above all that you have ever thought or asked when it comes to enriching your use of the disciplines of grace? Why or why not?

2. How much confidence do you have in prayer as a means of discovering God's will for your life in the practice of the disciplines of grace? Do you really expect him to show you areas for improvement? Are you open to whatever he might show you?

3. At this time, where do you expect God to speak to you about needed improvements in the practice of spiritual disciplines? Why do you feel this way?

4. What kinds of commitments do you think you will need to make in order to pursue those improvements and work out your salvation with the Lord? Are you prepared to make those commitments?

5. What would you like to see happening in your practice of the disciplines of grace that you currently are not experiencing? Do you really believe that God wants this for you? That he can provide it for you?

# 6

# a question of priorities

*"I don't have the time," we protest—instead of admitting that the proposal is not sufficiently important in our priorities to warrant taking the time for it. We always make time for things that are important enough.*
TED W. ENGSTROM & R. ALEC MACKENZIE

*So teach us to number our days, that we may apply our hearts unto wisdom.*
PSALM 90:12

*I* was a brand-new believer in Jesus Christ, fresh out of the chrysalis of misery, disappointment and frustration the Lord had wrapped around my life to create in me an openness to his grace. Full of the joy of my salvation and the release from guilt and condemnation that had hung over my head for years, I never struggled with the question of assurance; the Lord had promised to keep me unto himself, and I was persuaded that he could carry out that promise, no matter what happened in my life.

Or, for that matter, what didn't happen.

From the first days of my new life in Christ, Rick Duwe, the friend who had led me to the Savior, encouraged me in the practice of spiritual disciplines, especially the reading and study of God's Word and prayer. He had given me a Bible and showed me how, through the ACTS acronym (adoration, confession, thanksgiving and supplication), I could make prayer a regular part of my relationship with the Lord. He had tried to impress on me the importance of these disciplines as crucial to growing in the Lord and having the spiritual resources I would need to be able to deal with the trials and temptations I was sure to face.

I assured him that I understood how important these things were and, at first, made a good-faith effort to give them some place in my life. But I was so full of the joy of the Lord and the peace of God that I must have concluded that Bible reading and prayer were only for those who really needed it because I did not give them much of a place in my walk with the Lord.

From time to time I would run into Rick on campus, and he would ask, "Hey, T. M., how are you doing in your Bible reading and prayer? What are you learning? What requests have you seen the Lord begin to answer?" For a long time I put him off, saying that I was pretty busy and tired a lot of the time (since I was both a student and an athlete), and that I hadn't really had a chance to start these things, but I would as soon as I could. I promised.

One day Rick cornered me in the student union and took me off to the side. Again he asked about my practice of spiritual disciplines. And again I tried to put him off with the same lame answer. But this time I added, "I really do want to begin reading my Bible and praying, really." Rick responded without hesitating, "No, you don't." I laughed uneasily and replied, "Sure I do, and I promise, I'll get going on these things right away." "No you won't," came his heartless reply. By now I was beginning to be embarrassed and starting to feel a little agitated. I said, "Come on, Rick, what Christian doesn't want to read his Bible daily and have a good prayer life?" He looked me straight in the eye, poked his finger in my chest and said, "*You* don't." Then he put his arm around my shoulder and added, "T. M., we will do in our lives *only* and *exactly* what we want to do, and nothing else. And when you *really want* to begin having a consistent time of Bible study and prayer, you will. But not until then."

Those words sunk into my soul. It wasn't a question of whether I should. I certainly knew I should, even though I was so full of the joy and peace of God that I talked myself out of it whenever my conscience piqued me. It wasn't even a question of whether I had the time for Bible reading and prayer. I had as much time as anyone else did. Instead it was a question of whether I *wanted* to spend my time with the

Lord or to give it over to something of lesser consequence.

It was, in short, a question of priorities with respect to the use I made of my time.

Rick's words stung so deeply that, the very same day, I began setting aside time for the Lord. Changing my priorities meant changing my routines, beginning with how I used my time. I had to get up a little earlier each day at first, but the sacrifice of sleep was well worth it. God began a work in my life as a result of Rick's challenge, which has grown and expanded to become the sweetest occupation of my day.

But challenges and temptations have arisen over the years.

**Finding the Time**

We all experience those seasons of flatness when our time in the Word of God, prayer or any of the spiritual disciplines doesn't seem to yield the sense of God's glory and the transforming power of his grace that we expect and desire. Sometimes this can be because of the sovereign pleasure of God, as the *Westminster Confession of Faith* notes, when he for his own good reasons may be "withdrawing the light of His countenance, and suffering even such as fear him to walk in darkness and to have no light."[1] At such times there is nothing to do but to continue looking to him in prayer, waiting faithfully and obediently upon his grace to renew and revive us.

More often the problem is ours. But for most readers it will not be — as it was with me — that you are not spending any time at all with the Lord. It may be that you are not spending enough time with him. As Bill Hybels has noted, "Any way you cut it, a key ingredient in authentic Christianity is time. Not leftover time, not throwaway time, but quality time. Time for contemplation, meditation and reflection. Unhurried, uninterrupted time."[2]

Not that time in spiritual disciplines in and of itself has any particular value. The quality of time is more important than the quantity. However, adjusting your practice of the disciplines of grace by increasing the amount of time devoted to them can be a way to renewal. Spiritual disciplines need to be adjusted occasionally as we reach new levels of spiritual growth, encounter new challenges, have to deal with new temptations, and if we want our relationship with the Lord to continue growing and flourishing. If your practice of the disciplines of grace has not changed for many years, and if you are experiencing a certain flatness in them, they may have lapsed into mere routines, allowing you to maintain some kind of spiritual status quo in your life but not leading you to greater growth in the Lord.

One place to begin at such times is to consider whether or not you are spending enough time in the disciplines of grace on a daily basis. There are several reasons why this makes sense.

First, it makes sense because the more we come to know the Lord and grow in our love for him, the more time we will want to spend in his presence. When I first met Susie, my wife, I would look for ways of spending more time with her. We were both working at the same Christian camp, so I tried to make sure that we had all our meals together. I gave up time that I might have spent in other activities in order to be with her. I would even go out of my way during the course of the work day to drive by the section of the camp where I thought she might be working, just to be able to see her and exchange a greeting. After we were married, my desire to be with her only increased, and I set aside all my former friendships and diversions so that I could be at home with the woman I love.

So it is as we grow in love for the Lord. If in our times of spiritual discipline we are entering regularly into the arena of his power and grace, where the Word and Spirit are working to make his glory known and to transform us increasingly into the very image of Jesus Christ, we will want to spend more time in such activities. We'll look forward to those times as immensely satisfying, and we will delight in the presence of the Lord.

But if the time we are spending in spiritual disciplines has gone flat, if it is not yielding the encounter with the living God that it should, it may mean that we need to increase our time with the Lord so that we can get to know him—and ourselves—even better.

A second reason this makes sense is that we only have so much time in the day, and it may be that we are not using our time as wisely as we should. For example, it may surprise some of us to learn how much time we waste each week. I have "often taught time-management seminars to men and women in business. Such people are always looking for better ways to get more out of the day. One of the activities I take them through early on is an evaluation of their present time usage. I give them a 4" x 6"

card marked off into the days of the week and divided into half-hour seg-
ments, and I instruct them to keep track of their time for the coming
week. I also ask them to make a prediction as to what they will discover
about how much time they waste each week.

This challenge is usually greeted with scoffing and laughter. These are
busy and efficient business persons! They don't waste time! They con-
quer it! Just to humor me, I suppose, they agree to the exercise. At the
end of the week it never fails: nearly every participant is shocked to discover how much time he or she wastes each week—not just a few minutes here and there, but hours and hours of time wasted doing frivolous,
unproductive things, sitting at a desk daydreaming, mindlessly plunked
down in front of the television set or in any of a dozen other bona fide
time wasters.

The same is true of every one of us. Time is one of God's greatest gifts,
as Jonathan Edwards wrote: "Upon time we should set a high value, and
be exceeding careful that it be not lost; and we are therefore exhorted to
exercise wisdom and circumspection, in order that we may redeem it.
And hence it appears, that *time is exceeding precious*."[3]

We are called to make the most of our time (Eph 5:15-17). One way
of adding time to your day, therefore, is to try to discover the time wasters in your schedule and get rid of them, substituting in their place, perhaps, more time in the disciplines of grace.

Some years ago I decided to add more time for prayer and reading of
Scripture to my daily schedule. I began by tacking a little more time on at
the beginning and end of the day. I have always been able to get up a little earlier in the morning, if need be, so this was not a difficult change for
me. Staying up a little later at night, however, was another thing.

I had determined to add a time of Scripture reading and prayer by
myself just before going to bed. I would use that time to reflect on the
day just ending and to set my mind on the day ahead so that I could go to
sleep each night in the confidence that I had the Lord's perspective on
my activities and plans. For weeks I struggled with this. It seemed that,
by the time I was ready to be with the Lord, I was so tired that I just
could not concentrate, indeed, could barely keep my eyes open. I began
asking the Lord to help me get the victory over my weariness so that I
could increase my time with him.

It was not long, however, before the Lord showed me that it wasn't a matter of victory over weariness but over wastefulness—wastefulness of time.

I was watching the news before dinner one evening when two things were suddenly impressed on my mind. The first was that the news I was watching was familiar to me. I had heard it already on the radio during my thirty-minute drive home from the office. The second was that most of the evening news was spent in things I didn't need to hear—weather reports, local fluff, sports and commercials. So I got up and turned the television off, telling myself I'd catch the late news, just in case I missed anything important.

But that evening, as I watched first the 10:00 news, then the 11:00 news, I made the same two observations: I already knew most of this, and what I did not know was not really worth knowing anyway.

I calculated how much time I might be able to save if I allowed the news I listened to on the way to and from work each day, together with my reading of the paper and newsmagazines, to suffice. I decided I could cut out two hours a day of watching news—which, over the course of a week, amounts to fourteen hours, or, nearly two full working days. Surely I could find a better way to use this time than watching what I already knew and what was of no real value for my life in the kingdom of God. And surely some of that time could be devoted to the Lord in the practice of spiritual disciplines.

And it was. As a result, I have found that my evening devotions are becoming more important in my relationship with the Lord. If adding time on to the beginning or end of your day is not the answer, try considering whether you might carve some time out of the rest of your day by eliminating the time wasters that rob us of this precious gift from God.

**The Great Time Wasters**

Edwards wrote, "How little is the preciousness of time considered, and how little sense of it do the greater part of mankind seem to have! And to how little good purpose do many spend their time!"[4] This is true of many of us. While we are busy and active, we have little sense of where much of our time goes each day. And yet we never seem to have enough.

Undoubtedly some of our time—some of which could be devoted to the disciplines of grace—is gobbled up by one or more of the great time wasters. What are these great time wasters that rob us of precious moments that could be devoted to growing in the grace and knowledge of our Lord Jesus Christ?

*Television.* Far and away the first of the great time wasters is television. It is too easy to crash on the couch after a busy and tiring day and surf the networks for an entire evening, looking for whatever we think will afford us the greatest amount of diversion and entertainment. It is a temptation that many Christians find too difficult to resist.

Television is the greatest of time wasters for two reasons. First, most of what we watch on television does not contribute to our kingdom callings as followers of Christ. We might compare it with the hours of time people spent in the taverns in Edwards's day, "wasting away their hours in idle and unprofitable talk which will turn to no good account."[5] Television's content is mostly frivolous, amoral—or even immoral—comedy, high-tension drama, head-over-heals action or mere talk; but we would be hard-pressed to identify any meaningful, sustained way in which such programming makes us fitter vessels for the work of the Lord or any way in which it draws us closer to him.

And yet significant hours of our week are drained away in front of the television set, as Christians mindlessly soak up the world's agenda for the sake of a little cheap entertainment.

Second, television seems to have negative effects on how we live, as Neil Postman argues in his book *Amusing Ourselves to Death.*[6] This is especially true with respect to the way that we view religion. Television can make us less serious about our religion, both because it usually demeans or degrades it and because it promotes the idea that so many other matters are of so much more importance. The time we waste watching television is thus multiplied by the deleterious effects of television on our willingness and ability to engage in serious religious discussion with our neighbors and friends.[7]

This is not to say that television is all bad. Let's say, mostly bad. I simply want to call you to consider whether or not this greatest of time wasters has begun to erode and consume the moments of your life that might be better invested in disciplines of Christian growth.

*Avocations.* The second greatest thief in taking away our precious time from devotion to the Lord is surely our avocations. Avocations—sports, exercise, hobbies, fishing, hunting and other diversions—can be a source of great delight and welcome renewal. They can give rest to our minds, health to our bodies, even new vision and energy to our lives. But they can also become all-consuming passions that take us away from our real reason for being, which is to know the Lord and serve him in his kingdom.

I once knew a Christian leader who indulged a very serious hobby. It had begun harmlessly enough, just a way of bringing some excitement and joy to his life. But by the time I met him it had become an all-consuming passion, taking up enormous amounts of his time, a large space in his home, thousands and thousands of dollars, and huge amounts of energy. It may also have caused his ministry to suffer. I once talked with a man who was involved in the same ministry as this leader, and I asked if he knew him. "Oh, yes," he replied and began immediately to talk about the man's hobby. He even implied that the amount of time and focus he spent in his hobby was costing him credibility in his ministry and opportunities for greater service to the Lord. He agreed that the man had considerable gifts, but he lamented that his ministry seemed to get only the offscouring of his time, energy and focus.

Consider the etymology of the word *avocation*. The *a* means in the Latin "not." A *vocation* is a "calling," something we enter into out of a higher sense of purpose. Therefore, an avocation is, in many ways, "no calling." Avocations may well play a role in helping to fit us for our callings, as restful and delightful diversions that allow us time to refocus our vision and renew our strength for ministry. But all too often our avocations end up like the proverbial camel, crowding our tents and taking away room in our schedules for growth in grace and service to the Lord. And, as Simon Chan suggests, we may even subconsciously welcome our avocations as ways of avoiding the more rigorous, but more lasting, disciplines of growing in grace.[8] Edwards's advice on avocations is exceedingly sound:

> Such diversion is doubtless lawful; but for Christians to spend so much of their time, so many long evenings, in no other conversation than that which tends to divert and amuse, if nothing worse, is a sinful way of spending time, and tends to poverty of soul at least, if not to outward poverty.[9]

> Diversions should be used only in subserviency to business. So much, and no more, should be used, as doth most fit the mind and body for the work of our general and particular callings.[10]

*Work routines.* Many of us waste time at work, as my involvement in teaching time-management seminars showed me. We let certain mindless routines consume precious time on the job, some of which, as we shall see, can be captured for spiritual growth.

Activities like reading the mail, taking a break, going to lunch, responding to phone messages and ordering our work space are all important. But they can quickly become time wasters if we are not careful.

I have a terrible habit of opening my mail, scanning the contents, then setting it aside for later. I put my mail in one of the mountains of paper that loom around my workspace (I seem to work best when I feel as though everything is about to fall in on me). Sooner or later I screw up my resolve and work my way through one or more of those stacks. Many, if not most, of the things I work through I can simply throw away—invitations to subscribe to this or that journal, offers for free books if I join a book club, copies of e-mail or faxes following up some completed project or other, solicitations of various kinds. I had already taken the time to look at these items once. Now here I am doing it again, taking valuable moments of time in useless activities that could have been accomplished the first time around, leaving me free to spend my time on more productive matters. When will I ever learn? (My wife has just placed on my desk a little book entitled *Everything in Its Place: Conquering Paper Clutter.*[11] Do you think she's trying to tell me something?)

Work routines can gobble up time during the day, some of which we can put to use in the disciplines of Christian growth, helping us to redeem our time for the purposes of our kingdom callings in Christ.

*Daydreaming.* Everybody daydreams. We look out the window and let our eyes roam over the trees, traffic, skies or landscape while we think about nothing in particular, just breaking away for a few moments from whatever the task at hand may be. Or we lean back, close our eyes and think about where we will be over the weekend—the fishing trip, the excursion on the lake, the game of golf, the family picnic. We envision the people we will be with and think about how we would much rather be there now instead of where we happen to be. We may so zone out in the middle of some meeting or conversation that it takes two or three callings of our name to get our attention and bring us back to the business at hand.

Daydreaming is unavoidable. In fact, it can be quite enjoyable. It's one of the things that makes us uniquely human, this ability to transcend time and space through the imaginative regions of our minds. But the time spent daydreaming, while it is not bad, can be "improved," to use Edwards's term, if we recognize the opportunity for redeeming the time that daydreaming presents and if we discipline ourselves to use that time more constructively than as a mere diversion.

*Telephone.* Any of my friends will tell you that I hate the telephone. Very seldom will I ever initiate a call to anyone unless it relates to some matter of ministry or some urgent necessity (like the heat pump going on the blink, as it has today). I find it too easy, when I am on the phone, to let conversation drag on into all manner of things that are unrelated to the reason for the initial call. Some people can do five or six other things while they are on the phone. I'm not one of those. I have to give my full attention to the conversation, or I will get lost.

However, I suspect that many of the people who call me on the phone are that other type of person. While they are talking with me, they are involved in some business meeting, reviewing the remaining items on the agenda and dashing off a memo to some staff member, all the while filling the verbal space with things perhaps important to them but having nothing whatsoever to do with me. I have even heard people who, having called me on the phone, turn to an associate to give an instruction, then come back to me to explain what that was all about, at the same time saying something like "bear with me here while I just make a note of this." Meanwhile, I'm watching my computer lapse into rest phase, my train of thought is beginning to go off the tracks, and my irritation level is starting to rise. And why is it that, nine times out of ten, that kind of telephone conversation will be immediately followed by one from a nameless individual wanting me to switch my phone service?

Don't get me wrong; we could hardly get along without telephones. They are one of God's greatest technological innovations. Yet, like anything else, they can eat into our precious time, robbing us of moments that might be devoted to other business, allowing us to finish that business with enough time left for some involvement in spiritual disciplines.

*The Internet.* Some years ago I was working on an article on the American painter Andrew Wyeth. I had read a number of books and visited the Brandywine River Museum in Chadds Ford, Pennsylvania, and I was looking for an angle into what I wanted to say. I decided to surf the Net a bit to see what I could find.

This is not as easy as it purports to be. My initial search yielded some three hundred thousand sites concerned with the name *Andrew Wyeth*. Dutifully, I began looking at some of them. The first sixty or seventy yielded nothing of any value for my research; however, I was persuaded that the very next site would be the one I wanted. This went on for what seemed like hours (I was new to the Internet at the time, and although I tried various combinations of key words, I still kept coming up with far too many sites to visit). My search was interrupted suddenly by a message popping up on my screen out of nowhere. It was my son, Kevin, who had noticed that I was online and decided to send me an instant message, which led to a not-so-instant virtual conversation, distracting me from my research (which was going nowhere) and leading me to think that I ought to check my e-mail.

So I went over to my e-mail and read through the many letters in my box, including all those forwarded from well-meaning friends and family who were forwarding to me things forwarded to them by others to whom they had been forwarded. I replied to some of the e-mail, deleted much of the rest and saved some for Susie to read, and by the time I was done, an entire evening was gone.

What did I have to show for over four hours of time on the Internet? A few e-mails sent to friends and family, a nice chat with my son (who lived twenty minutes from us), and a lot of wasted attention and energy on frivolous, unfruitful activities.

I was so tired I went straight to bed.

Many of us have no doubt experienced the frustration of using the Internet, trying to keep up with our e-mail, or just exploring this vast entanglement of cyber venues in order to learn a little more about what's out there. If so, you know just how quickly and easily the Internet can eat up precious time.

*Sleeping.* Solomon had the right take on sleep:

A little sleep, a little slumber,
  a little folding of the hands
      to rest,
and poverty will come upon you
      like a robber,
    and want, like an armed warrior. (Prov 24:33-34 NRSV)

I have been told that people need eight hours of sleep each night in order to maintain health and humor. I have never found that to be true for me. Certainly there is no biblical prescription to that effect, and I'm not sure the scientific community could demonstrate it beyond a doubt. Yet how many of us dutifully stretch out for our recommended daily dose of sleep, taking away from valuable time that might be invested in spiritual growth? Or how many of us have fallen into habits or patterns of sleep that have remain unchanged for years, that is, never adjusted to make more time for other things, including spiritual disciplines?

Great saints in the Bible were famous for sleeplessness, for wrestling with God in prayer and solitude while the great majority of saints lay comfortably in their beds. Consider David: "I am weary with my moaning; / every night I flood my bed with tears; / I drench my couch with my weeping" (Ps 6:6 NRSV); and Asaph: "You keep my eyelids from closing; / I am so troubled that I cannot speak" (Ps 77:4 NRSV); and Paul: "In toil and hardship, through many a sleepless night" (2 Cor 11:27 NRSV). Just as many were the saints who cut their sleep short in order to be with the Lord before the break of day such as Abraham (Gen 19:27) and the Lord Jesus (Mk 1:35). I suspect that these great leaders would have scoffed at the idea that they had to get eight hours of sleep every night. They would no doubt have said, "How can I afford to sleep so long, when there is so much to talk with the Lord about, so many challenges for which to prepare, and when my soul needs so much refreshment in the presence of God?"

Could it be that some of the time we ought to be investing in growing stronger in the Lord is being wasted in too much sleep? How will we ever know if we never challenge our bodies to do without a little sleep in order to spend more time in the presence of the Lord of glory? We are called to bring our bodies into subjection for the purpose of our callings in Christ (1 Cor 9:24-27). Certainly sleep has a place in that. How much sleep is the question each of us needs to consider, for it may be that, with a little more self-discipline, we could relinquish a half-hour or an hour of sleep each day for the purpose of devoting our souls to more refreshment in the disciplines of grace.

### Taking Stock

All of us waste time now and then. That's not such a big deal. But it becomes a problem when wasting time becomes part of every day and when we aren't aware of the ways that wasted time can creep into our daily activities. At least some of that wasted time can be redeemed for the practice of spiritual disciplines. But unless we take the time to examine our time and seek the grace of God for wisdom in how we might use that time better (Ps 90:12), we won't be able to recover it for spiritual renewal. One place to move from routine to renewal is increasing the amount of time we spend in the practice of spiritual disciplines. Adjusting our daily routines by eliminating wasted time and devoting at least some of those recovered moments to the disciplines of grace can help us to get back on track for renewal in the Lord.

### Questions for Study or Discussion

1. Approximately how much time do you spend in the practice of spiritual disciplines each day? Do you feel that this is adequate to help you grow in the Lord? Why or why not?

2. If you could recover some time each day for spiritual disciplines, which ones would you most likely increase? How would you expect to benefit from this?

3. Do you recognize any of the great time wasters in your own life? Which ones? Have they reached the problem stage in your life as relates to the practice of spiritual disciplines?

4. Spend some time in prayer over your use of time. Meditate on Ephesians 5:15-17. Why does Paul stress the importance of "redeeming the time" in this passage?

5. Try to identify some ways of recovering at least thirty minutes of lost time each day. Where would you look? Do you believe that the Lord can help you recover that time for the purpose of spiritual renewal?

# 7

# Redeeming the Time

*To follow Jesus came to mean, for the early disciples, what it must inevitably mean for a follower in any age—not an encounter for personal gain, but an act of self-losing for those gains which are of a spiritual nature, and of such self-giving consequence that they, as his followers, allow him to state the terms of their devotion and of their sacrifice.*
JOHN E. GARDNER

*See then that ye walk circumspectly, not as fools, but as wise, Redeeming the time, because the days are evil.*
EPHESIANS 5:15-16

*O*nce you have identified the areas of your life where you are wasting precious time, you will need to resolve to recover at least some of that time for the practice of spiritual disciplines. Make this a matter of devoted prayer, seeking the strength and guidance of the Lord in firming up that resolve. Ask your prayer partner or Bible study group to support you in prayer in this effort. Once the priority of gaining more time for the disciplines of grace becomes firmly established, you will be in a position to seek the Lord's counsel and strength to begin making those changes, eagerly expecting him to bring renewal to your life as you do.

Jonathan Edwards wrote about the importance of working to "improve" our time spent in spiritual disciplines—what he called "holy time": "Be especially careful to improve *those parts* of time which are most precious. Though all time is very precious, yet some parts are more precious than others; as, particularly, holy time is more precious than common time."[1] We can improve this holy time, at least in part, through increasing the amount of time spent in spiritual disciplines, not just during our times of devotion, but throughout the day, as we learn how to recover wasted time for investment in spiritual renewal.

Edwards urged his congregation on in this effort, admonishing them in the use of their time to "Lose it not in sleep, or in carelessness, inattention, and wandering imaginations."[2] In other words, not to waste their time but to use it as much as possible for their callings as followers of the Lord.

Taking back wasted time will be hard work, as will carving out a little more time in the day for spiritual disciplines, but if our disciplines have fallen into mere routines, this can be a good place to start. Not everyone enjoys equal success in this approach to moving from routine to renewal; we don't all waste the same amount of time each day. And merely recovering more time for the practice of spiritual disciplines will not necessarily ensure that that time is spent in anything more than more spiritual routines. Still, if you have discovered that wasted time is one of the obstacles you have to overcome in moving from routine to renewal, at least some of the suggestions that follow should be of help.

I was once told that if you have to swallow a frog, don't spend too much time looking at it; and if you have to swallow a lot of frogs, start with the big one. It's probably the case that, in moving from routine to renewal in the practice of spiritual disciplines, we all have a lot of frogs to swallow. The big frog for many of us may well be those time wasters discussed in the previous chapter. And while swallowing that big frog may be a hefty challenge, we can look to the Lord to help us as we bring our lives more into line with our renewed priorities. Once you have identified the time wasters in your life, you'll need to develop a strategy for overcoming them. Only then will you be in a position to know just how much new time can be redeemed for the practice of spiritual disciplines. Prayerfully consider each of the following suggestions as you wait on the Lord to guide and empower you for renewal in your spiritual life.

### Attacking the Time Wasters

If you cannot gain control of the great time wasters in your life, you are not going to add much time for spiritual disciplines to your day. Time wasters are like dandelions: they seem harmless enough, but before you know it, they have grown and expanded and covered the whole place, smothering your schedule and stifling productivity and growth. So if we can discipline ourselves to attack the time wasters, overcoming at least some of the things that rob us of precious minutes and hours, we'll be in a position to talk seriously about increasing the time we have available for spiritual disciplines. Let me make some suggestions.

*Television.* One of my favorite John Denver songs is titled "Blow Up Your TV." While such advice may not be practical, I think you get the point: We do not need to watch as much TV as many of us do.

Why not try cutting back on the amount of TV you watch? Start with the big frog—your favorite program. Let it go for a week, then two, then a month. Then drop one additional program each week until you have discovered how unimportant TV is to your walk with the Lord and how much time you can free up for more productive activities. Take the batteries out of your remote control and stick them in a drawer in another room. That way you will avoid mindlessly turning the TV on and sitting down to channel surf. Put your TV in a different place, one less convenient to where you like to sit. Ask a family member or prayer partner to hold you accountable for watching less TV. Tell him or her what you are planning to cut out this week, and then let that family member pray for you and encourage you. And if all that fails, John Denver's advice might not be such a bad idea.

Time recovered from sitting in front of the television can then be put to use in the disciplines of grace. Not all of it, certainly, but enough to allow your sails to know the Spirit's lively breezes, so that you move out of the doldrums of routine into renewal once again.

*Avocations.* Second, make your avocations serve your vocation—your calling as a citizen of the kingdom of God. If you like fishing, learn to use part of that time for being alone with the Lord. Make a point to pray reflectively on the beauty of your surroundings or to work on Scripture memorization. If golfing is your game, make a prayer partner of your golf buddy and light up the links together with praise, thanks and spiritual encouragement of one another as you make your way to the clubhouse. Maybe exercise is your thing. Instead of listening to disco tapes while you exercise, try praise songs, with the intention of learning to sing them in your heart as you workout; or listen to Scripture tapes to focus your thoughts on the Lord and help improve your Scripture memory.

Obviously it doesn't take a lot to bring the presence of the Lord into our avocations. We just need to be willing to do so and set our minds to the challenge. Ask a friend or prayer partner for suggestions in this area and make yourself accountable for specific activities. If you do, the Lord will guide and reward you as you commit to redeeming some of your avocational time for spiritual growth.

*Daydreams.* Third, capture your daydreams for spiritual growth and ministry. Daydreams usually begin with our thinking of something or someone beyond our immediate space or somewhere we would rather be than where we are. The apostle Paul found his mind would wander from time to time, often to some of the people he loved and served in ministry. When that happened, he took it as a cue from the Lord to come into his presence in prayer, as he wrote to the Philippians: "I thank my God for you every time you come to mind" (Phil 1:3, my paraphrase). Daydreams give us an excellent, albeit brief, opportunity to expand our prayers of thanks, praise and intercession simply by taking the subject of the daydream and making it the focus of prayer. By doing so, what would normally be time wasted can become time invested for spiritual growth and renewal.

Perhaps you are daydreaming about the weekend at the lake coming up next month. Praise and thank the Lord for the beauty of his world, for the work that allows you time away and sufficient income for such a retreat and for the people with whom you will be together at that time. With a little imagination and discipline, all our daydreams can similarly be brought into the service of helping to redeem your time for spiritual disciplines.

*Work routines and phoning.* Next, schedule your work routines. Simple but important routines like going through the mail, returning phone calls and setting up meetings can all be done at the same time each day and usually within a fairly limited space of time. If you plan time for these activities, you won't be tyrannized by their hanging over your head, and they won't accumulate in such numbers that they overwhelm you and rob you of precious time during the day, some of which might be given over to the disciplines of grace.

In the same way, do your phoning all at once. If you have twenty phone calls to make, set a time each day to make them. That way they won't stack up on you. When the time is up, put the phone away and go on to something else. You won't have that many calls tomorrow, and you can catch up then. If any call you were not able to return is really urgent, you can expect the person who called to call you again. Set time during the day when you refuse to take phone calls and devote some of that time to spiritual disciplines—meditation, Scripture memorization or praying a psalm.

*Internet and e-mail.* Treat your e-mail as extended conversation. Answer e-mails with brief phrases just as you would in a conversation, not like a letter, where you want to fill in more details and cover more topics. I delete all forwarded e-mail, especially if I'm one of a string with many others. Rarely have I found forwarded e-mail to be anything other than a waste of time. In one ministry I know of, the director of information technology has programmed the server to delete all e-mail forwarded to all members of the staff. Don't let e-mail become a substitute for face-to-face conversation or more considered correspondence, and don't try to do too much via this wonderful time waster. Keep it short. Check it once or twice daily only. And fight the temptation to surf the Net without a clear purpose and a narrow field for your search.

*Sleeping.* Finally, see if you can cut back on sleep. Not everyone will be able to do this and not to the same extent. You'll never know if you can until you try. But you need to give it a couple of weeks. One or two days of setting your alarm fifteen or thirty minutes earlier or going to bed later won't prove anything, whether or not you are able to do it. Two weeks begins to establish a new sleep pattern and frees up time to expand your spiritual disciplines so that they become more regular and significant.

Don't try to cut back on sleep dramatically. Start with just fifteen or thirty minutes, taken off either at the morning or at night. If that seems to work OK, you can increase it. But make sure that you commit some of the time recovered from sleep for the practice of the disciplines of grace. Don't get up fifteen minutes early only to squander that additional time perusing the paper or looking at morning news shows. Get right to the task for which you are trying to recover this time and come into the presence of the Lord, seeking his glory and power.

## Devoting Recovered Time to Spiritual Disciplines

As you redeem some of the time currently given to time wasters, you will find that you have more time available each day, some of which can be devoted to spiritual disciplines. But this will not guarantee that the time you have recaptured will be put to this use. Remember, the devil has plenty of seemingly harmless, even important ways of diverting you from this important calling. You'll need to make a conscious effort to convert time wasted to time invested for spiritual growth.

Some of your spiritual disciplines will expand naturally as you capture precious moments for holy time throughout the day, such as during your brief periods of daydreaming or in the time recovered from sleeping a little less. The more you snag and fill these times with disciplines of grace, the more they will become a habitual and meaningful part of your daily life. You will be reluctant to yield up your time to those old, banished time wasters ever again.

*Plan specific daily activities.* But it would be helpful in seeking to expand your disciplines to plan for specific, new or expanded spiritual exercises at different times of the day. For example, if you are accustomed to having your devotions in the morning, add a fifteen-minute devotional in the evening as well (or the other way around). Begin or increase your work in Scripture memorization. Carry Scripture cards with you during the day or commit to learning a whole book of the Bible by heart (I think I'd start with 3 John). Use some of the time you are recovering during the day to review your memory work and to thank the Lord for his Word and the grace of a healthy mind.

*Set times for prayer.* If you feel adventuresome, you might try scheduling different periods for prayer during the day—say, one at midmorning, one at noon, one in the afternoon and one after the evening meal. Not long seasons of intercession, just ten- or twelve-minute periods to give thanks and praise to God for the day, the people on your mind, and the work already completed, and to prepare yourself spiritually for the rest of the day ahead.

The saints of the Old and New Testaments kept set hours of prayer, and we are no busier than they were (after all, Daniel administered an entire empire [Dan 6:10], and Peter and John were pastors in a megachurch [Acts 3:1]). During the period of the early church it was the practice of Christians from many walks of life to observe these set hours of prayer. Tertullian, for example, recommended keeping the hours of 9:00 a.m., noon and 3:00 p.m., in addition to rising and retiring, as set times for prayer.[3] Surely some of the time we have recovered by attacking our time wasters can be reconfigured to accommodate brief seasons of prayer during the day.

It is not necessary to retire to some private prayer closet at such times. Take a few moments at your desk, while the kids are napping or as you are walking to class, and focus on the Lord. Let the things around you guide your prayer or the passage of Scripture you are working to memorize. What's important is to set aside regular time where you discipline your mind and heart to focus on the Lord rather than allowing it to meander aimlessly, waiting for whatever comes next.

*Schedule a day of fasting.* Schedule a day of fasting each month. Since I'll have more to say about fasting in a later chapter, I'll leave it at this for now. Fasting once a month—or once a week—can be a wonderful way of drawing closer to the Lord and of knowing the power of his sustaining grace. But you have to plan and prepare for it.

*Plan an hour of solitude.* Try to grab an hour of solitude each week, when you draw away from everything routine in your life to concentrate on being with the Lord. It doesn't have to be the same time each week or even in the same place. You can even combine solitude and fasting by skipping lunch one day, going to a park or museum, and focusing on the goodness of the Lord in prayer.

*Evaluate your use of the Lord's Day.* For many Christians the Lord's Day can become a catchall of wasted time without their even knowing it. From the creation the Lord set this day apart for himself so that we might cease from our normal activities and devote time meditating on and resting in him and his various works (Gen 2:1-3; Ex 20:8-11; Is 58:13-14). As we do so, we will find the spiritual refreshment and renewal that the Lord intended for us in this day (Mk 2:27-28).

But it is very easy for our sabbath to become filled with activities that draw us away from the Lord rather than allow us to rest in him—things like shopping, avocations, sports, television and a host of others. Take a look at your own use of this valuable spiritual resource: Is it filled with activities that focus your affections on the Lord, or has a crowd of time wasters been robbing you of that spiritual refreshment? Begin cutting back on distractions and putting in place activities that will enable you to realize the renewing grace of God on this day, and you will find that the Lord's Day can become an important ongoing source of renewal in your life.

I know these last two chapters sound a lot like a time-management seminar, but the key to being able to expand your time in spiritual disciplines is identifying wasted time and redeeming at least some for concentrated engagement with the Lord. This must not be an occasional undertaking but an exercise of continuous vigilance on our parts, an ongoing matter of prayer and seeking the will of God. This way we will always be sure that we are exercising the best possible stewardship of our time and that we have as much time as possible to devote to being in the presence of our God.

### Be Accountable for Your Time

Edwards advises us to remember:

> You are accountable to God for your time. Time is a talent given us by God; he hath set us our day; and it is not for nothing, our day was appointed for some work; therefore he will, at the day's end, call us to an account. We must give account to him of the improvement of all our time.[4]

It never fails to amaze me how quickly my precious time can become wasted. But I have discovered that I can keep this process in check by maintaining a constant accountability for my time, making sure daily that it is being put to the best possible use—especially for the practice of spiritual disciplines.

I have found three practices helpful in exercising a meaningful and effective accounting of my time. It is not my purpose to recommend that you follow my procedure; rather, I simply want to stimulate your own thinking about devising some effective way of keeping track of your time—"numbering" your days, as Moses would have it (Ps 90:12).

*Keep track of your time.* First, I try to keep track of how I use my time throughout the day. This involves recording in a journal how I spend the time that the Lord gives me each day. I do this by noting in a brief phrase or two what I did during the block of time just ended. After my morning devotions I record the passages read and usually a thought or two in reflection on them. After that I clean up and get ready for the day. Then I normally move to a session of writing, at the end of which I record in my journal the project I was working on and the particular type of writing (first draft, revision, final edit, etc.) that I was doing. I keep this up throughout the day so that at the end of the day I have a record of how all my waking moments were spent. I'm not obsessive about this. OK, I am obsessive—but that doesn't mean you have to be. I simply want to encourage you to find some way of being more aware of your time and the way you use it.

This has two advantages. First, it makes me constantly mindful of how my time is spent throughout the day. Yes, I even record the time that I waste in some frivolous or nonproductive activity, which forces me to face up to my lack of stewardship for those lost moments. Besides a stab of conviction, this normally has the effect of stirring up my resolve to do better with the rest of my time that day. Second, keeping track of my time provides a written record to review in prayer at the end of the day so that I am able to thank the Lord for the work accomplished, seek his forgiveness for any wasted time and prepare myself before him for the day ahead. This kind of personal accountability for my time has become so much a part of my personal ethic that I find it neither cumbersome nor tedious. On the contrary, it is usually a source of great satisfaction and encouragement, as well as a stimulus to reflective prayer and praise.

*Be accountable to someone for spiritual discipline.* Second, try to have someone who will help to hold you accountable for the time you invest in the disciplines of grace. I'll have more to say about this in a later chapter, but let me offer just a few remarks at this point.

As it relates to spiritual disciplines, you should have someone who receives a regular accounting of your devotional time. In my case, this begins with my wife, Susie. At some point most days we share with one another from our reading and study of Scripture and spend some time in prayer. It is important to me to hear from her what the Lord has been showing her in his Word and to have her respond to my impressions of what he is saying to me. In addition to Susie, I have found it beneficial over the years to meet with another man or two for the same purpose, sharing with them my journey with the Lord and joining with them in prayer for the concerns in each of our lives. Just knowing that I have a standing commitment to share with other people helps motivate me to greater faithfulness and more attentiveness in the practice of spiritual disciplines.

Just this morning I spoke by phone with Brian Bankard, a business-
man and one of my soul friends, and we shared together from what the
Lord was teaching us in our study of the Gospel of Matthew (we use the
same Scripture Union devotional materials). We were also able to swap
prayer requests and encourage one another in our various ministry activities. The fact that Brian lives on Maryland's Eastern Shore while I'm in
the heart of Appalachia has not impeded our ability to continue holding
one another accountable and encouraging one another in the practice of
spiritual disciplines.

*Be accountable to the Lord for your time.* Finally, each of us needs to find
some ways of being accountable to the Lord for our time. With me, this
comes during my times of planning and my review of the way I used my
time during the day.

I find it useful to review my personal statement of mission and vision
on an annual basis. From there I can set my goals for the year. Since
these include goals for spiritual growth, they provide a focus for my studies and prayers for the entire year. During the course of the year, as I
take on various projects and enter into diverse activities, I take time to
plan and set goals for each of them. Then I will plan my week—which
projects to work on and how much to get done—and each day of the
week, prioritizing the things I need to work on or get done for each day.
All of this time is spent before the Lord with Psalm 90:12 in the forefront
of my brain, reminding me that God has to teach me how to number my
days and give me the wisdom and strength to do what he leads me to put
on my schedule.

For many people, planning is a tedious, unhappy business. It takes
time and can be frustrating. They prefer to jump into each day and take
whatever comes. Of course, we all do this to a certain extent. None of
our plans are infallible—our "best laid plans," as Robbie Burns reminded
us, "gang aft aglee"—and each of us is susceptible to the pull and tug of
unanticipated eventualities. Yet those who take the time to plan their
lives are not only more likely to get where they want to be, but also their
planning can afford a wonderful opportunity for being before the Lord—
in meditation, prayer and solitude—as they wait upon him to counsel and
advise them concerning the mundane realities of their lives.

At the end of each day, project and month, I spend some time in meditation and prayer before the Lord, seeking input from his Spirit con-

cerning the time I have invested for him. Sometimes he will bring to mind things I could have done better or perhaps should not have done at all. Other times I think I hear him saying, "Well, done," and this fills me with a great sense of satisfaction. At still other times I may suddenly be led to see a new or better way of doing something, a way through some impasse that has been blocking me, or a new idea worth exploring.

It is important for me to review my time before the Lord with an open mind and heart so that I can have some degree of assurance that my "labor is not in vain" before him (1 Cor 15:58 NRSV).

One way to begin restoring your spiritual disciplines is to add more time for them in your daily schedule. By increasing our disciplines we will not only be making a better investment of our time, we also will find our concentration heightened and a greater and more consistent sense of being in the Lord's presence. Getting a better handle on our time is the key, which we can do if we recognize this great gift for what it is, take steps to identify wasted time and determine to redeem it, and convert some of that time to the practice of spiritual disciplines.

## Questions for Study or Discussion

1. Have you identified any wasted time in your daily routines? Where?

2. What advantages might you expect to realize from redeeming some of that time for the practice of spiritual disciplines? What obstacles do you face?

3. Who could help keep you accountable for better use of your time, especially in the practice of spiritual disciplines? How might you work together to encourage one another in this effort?

4. Did any of the suggestions in this chapter for redeeming wasted time strike you as workable for you? Which? How might you implement those suggestions?

5. Merely adding more time to the practice of spiritual disciplines will not guarantee that you move from routine to renewal in these special arenas of grace. Are you able to identify any other obstacles in your practice of spiritual disciplines that you will need to address for that to happen?

# 8

# intensifying the time

*The yield of our life does not depend so much on the number of things that we do,*
*but more on the quality of self-giving that we put to each thing.*
PAUL TOURNIER

*I will not let thee go, except thou bless me.*
GENESIS 32:26

*I* am a casual bird-watcher. That is, I find great delight in observing the various feathered friends who gather at our birdfeeders throughout the year. They are, for me, a living display of the glory, beauty, variety and wonder of the living God and lead me to praise and thank him often.

Almost anyone can distinguish certain kinds of birds at a glance. A robin is easy to identify, as are cardinals, blue jays and crows. But it takes more preparation, concentration and time to distinguish between various other birds. Sparrows, for example. Anyone can look out at a small, buff-colored bird sitting on a wire and rightly identify it as a sparrow. But what kind of sparrow? Around our home four kinds of sparrows make their nests and feed. Only by looking intently at any individual bird is it possible to discern the differences between them and appreciate their individual beauty.

Even with birds of the same species it is possible to distinguish individuals by carefully noting such things as size, behavior and relationship to others of their kind. Our hummingbird feeder, for example, hangs below a bough of a young maple tree in our front yard. Three particular hummers routinely avail themselves of the sweet liquid I prepare for them. They are so different from one another in their coloring and behavior that we have given them names. Ruby, the female, is smaller, less spectacular in coloring and tends to drink from all the cups at the feeder. Ruvy, the dominant male, likes to perch on a limb above the feeder, keeping an eye on things and determining, by his often-aggressive behavior, who will feed when. Rudy, the other male, is clearly in submission to Ruvy and never challenges his authority but drinks only when he is allowed to do so. Their individual characteristics are clearly identifiable, but to notice them you have to look more closely. When you do, this greatly enhances the beauty they display and wonder that they provide.

The key in getting the most out of watching birds is to know what you are looking for and to cultivate the discipline of intently observing each individual representative that comes into your purview. I never fail to delight in the ever-deepening layers of the glory of God that I see revealed in the attributes and habits of the birds that gather around our feeders.

The same is true of the practice of spiritual disciplines. We have discussed at some length what our goals and expectations ought to be from the practice of spiritual disciplines—what we ought to be looking for. We come to this time in order to meet with the living God, to encounter him in the power of his Spirit and Word in life-changing ways, so that we might grow in love for him and for our neighbors. We also discussed the necessity of preparing ourselves to come to the disciplines with the outlook of a lively faith if we are actually going to meet with God and know the transforming power of his Spirit and Word at work in our lives.

In the previous chapter we considered the possibility of increasing the amount of time spent in spiritual disciplines as a way to move from routine to renewal. But I also warned against thinking that merely increasing your time in the disciplines of grace will accomplish what you seek. Unless you make better use of your time in those special arenas of grace, no amount of increased activity will make any difference. Part of what is involved in making better use of your time is learning how to intensify your involvement with spiritual disciplines, to concentrate more deeply, observe more carefully and reflect at deeper levels.

In this chapter I suggest some ways of moving from routine to renewal through various activities that can intensify your focus and enrich your participation in the disciplines. The suggestions mentioned below can be applied, with adaptations, to other spiritual disciplines as well. Not all of them will appeal to you. However, others and I have found these suggestions to be helpful at one point or another in our own spiritual journeys over the years.

## Intensifying the Discipline of God's Word

In preceding chapters I have suggested two practices that can help us have a more intensive and personal encounter with the living God in the disciplines of his Word: journaling and sharing with others. By keeping a journal or other written record of our reading and study in which we reflect, raise questions and write out personal applications from our study, we allow the Lord to impress the teaching of his Word more deeply on our lives and have a record for future review and assessment. Further, sharing what we read and learn from God's Word with another person on a regular basis can have a similar effect. Either, if not both, of these is a good place to start in intensifying your time in the discipline of God's Word.

*Journaling.* As you read, journaling can be a very rewarding practice. In his helpful little book *Spiritual Journaling: Recording Your Journey Toward God*, Richard Peace observes:

> Journaling is, itself, a spiritual discipline. It focuses mind and heart on the issues of growth with the aim of discerning what God is doing in one's life. By using a journal, we come in touch with our cutting edges of growth, those areas where questions exist or where there is need or longing. These are the areas where the Holy Spirit often seems most active.
>
> Journaling is also an aid to other spiritual disciplines. Writing down your insights is helpful in Bible study. Writing out prayers helps you to communicate with God. Creating a poem that praises God is an act of worship. Journaling with others and sharing your work is a way to create Christian community.[1]

There are many different ways to approach journaling. You might try isolating just one or two verses from your reading, then make some written observations about the central teaching of this passage using a few simple questions to guide your thinking. Ask what the main idea in the passage is, what this teaching means for you, how you might apply it that day and what would be different in your life if you did. Make a few summary comments to firm up your conclusions and sharpen the focus of your thinking. Don't worry too much about proper grammar or spelling; just let your responses flow, trying to get down as many thoughts as you can in a brief space and time. From time to time during the day pause to think about what you read during your devotions and review your written response. Ask the Lord to show you opportunities to put the teaching of his Word into practice, and then faithfully follow as he leads.

I have often found such an exercise to yield immediate benefits in my daily life. For example, not long ago I made the following observation in my journal from Ephesians 3:19:

> Paul says that the love of Christ surpasses knowledge, but that we indeed may know his love. He seems to say that the love of Christ is more than some kind of merely intellectual experience. Instead, it goes beyond that to something more intensely personal that we experience in our hearts, souls, minds, and all of life, and that makes us more like Christ in our relationships with others. Only when we know the love of Christ in this way will we begin to be filled with all the fullness of God. Lord, let Your love—and my love for You—capture me throughout, in all my being, that I may know more of Your fullness in me!

I spent some moments meditating on how I might immediately come to know the love of Christ more fully in my life that day, and I asked the Lord to point me to some clear opportunities for showing his love to others. After a busy morning of writing, phone calls and errands I returned to prayer just before lunch and turned to my journal to reflect again on the teaching of this passage. It occurred to me as I was meditating on my comments that I could act on what I had read right away by taking the time to fix lunch for my wife, Susie, and to sit with her while she ate. Since I work at home, this is easy enough to do, but it did require an adjustment in my schedule, setting aside my work for an hour or so. It was a simple gesture but very much appreciated, and it resulted in our sharing a delightful time together in the Lord. We had a lively conversation as she ate her lunch, and we were able to discuss a family matter of some urgency and come to a clear resolution as to how we should deal with it. We ended our time in prayer together, then went about our separate business again, and I enjoyed the deep-seated satisfaction of knowing that Christ had overridden my natural self-centeredness to show his love through me in this small but meaningful way. I'm certain that none of this would have ensued without that time of more intense observation of Paul's teaching, together with later reflection on it.

I like to enter in the margin of my Bible the date on which I journal on a text of Scripture. By doing this, the next time I come to that passage or when I might be preparing to teach it, I can easily consult my diary to reflect afresh on what the Lord taught me previously and then add to that understanding whatever he may be pleased to show me on this subsequent reading. Journaling as you read the Word of God can be a most helpful way of intensifying your time in Scripture and helping you to come into the presence of God more fully. Journaling can help you to focus more sharply, reflect more deeply and apply the Scriptures more personally.

*Sharing with others.* Sharing in God's Word with a friend is another way of intensifying your encounters with him there. Steven Wright is one of my *anamcara* or "soul friends." For a number of years we lived in the same community, and it was our practice from time to time to meet together once a week in the study of God's Word. We would share from our devotions or discuss a book we were reading together. During one period we were studying the book of Galatians for our devotions, then coming together to share our findings and encourage one another in the Lord. At that time I was involved in some ecumenical discussions in which a group of theologians and church leaders was trying to hammer out a statement on justification by faith that representatives of a wide range of Christian communions could affirm together. The discussions were difficult and prolonged and at times confusing as we tried to understand one another and reach language that we could all agree on. My studies in Galatians with Steven were most helpful during that time, as we would frequently discuss the importance of seeking unity on the basis of truth and not merely for its own sake. Steven would question me about my involvement in this ecumenical effort, about our purpose and the wording of our statement, and he cautioned me to do everything in my power to keep our group from, in the name of unity, declaring another gospel (Gal 1:6-10). His insights were often penetrating, and his questions helped to clarify my thinking. My understanding of Paul's letter was deepened, and our time together was richly rewarding, both in my personal faith and in my involvement with this ecumenical effort.

There are other ways of sharing with another person in the discipline of God's Word. In my household we often spend a portion of Sunday afternoons sharing together from our time in Scripture from the previous week. Susie and I—and, at times, various of our children when they are able to be with us—encourage one another, clarify unclear passages and relate them to other portions of the Word of God, and enjoy the rich fellowship of the grace God has shown to each of us.

*Using guides to Scripture.* Another approach to intensifying your time in the Word of God is to make use of reliable guides. Here I do not have in mind the kind of study booklets that require you to answer questions on a text of Scripture. As useful as these can be, they are most helpful when used in a context of group study or with a friend, such as Steven Wright and I have done. Rather, I am thinking of those devotional and other guides that walk the reader through a text of Scripture, teaching and applying the Word of God in specific ways.

For example, I have found the Ancient Christian Commentary on Scripture published by InterVarsity Press to be an insightful guide during my morning devotions. This series brings together comments from the fathers of the early church in a verse-by-verse explication of whole books of the Bible. In spite of the sometimes-allegorizing perspectives they present, the writers never fail to stimulate my thinking and enlighten my understanding in ways that just reading the biblical text does not quite attain. I have found that much of what the fathers observed confirms my own understanding of Scripture or opens up new horizons on the text that I might otherwise never have seen. At such times I experience a deep sense of the oneness of the body of Christ throughout the ages and am drawn more closely to the Lord who reigns over his people in all times. The comments of these great saints from the formative years of the church have become an increasingly important part of my morning devotions.

Other types of commentaries can be helpful as well. My friend Ken Nordstrom finds the commentaries of Matthew Henry valuable in pointing out new insights into familiar passages of God's Word. He also uses the printed sermons of his pastor, Dr. D. James Kennedy, as a way or reviewing what he heard and going deeper into the text that was the subject of the sermon. The Scripture Union devotional guides can also be a source of reliable teaching through the Word of God on a systematic basis.

You may not always agree with what these different guides teach, and sometimes you will see things in the text that are more important for you than the matters the writers have addressed. You will need to wrestle with God at such times, like Jacob holding tightly until he was blessed, seeking from him a clearer understanding or more relevant application of the text to your life. By using such guides and wrestling with the Scriptures more deeply, you may receive new insights and be presented with new challenges as you seek to follow Jesus each day.

These are just a few ways that you can make your time in the discipline of God's Word more intensive and personal. You may need to add a little time to your schedule for reading and studying God's Word, but it will be well worth it in the encounter with God and the growth in grace that you experience.

### Intensifying the Discipline of Prayer

In the previous chapter I mentioned some ways that, by increasing the amount of time allotted to prayer, you could increase the intensity of your prayers as well. Here I want to mention three other practices that can help to make your prayers a richer experience of encountering the living God.

*Written prayers.* As part of my journaling I try to include a brief, written prayer to the Lord concerning the teaching of the text. As Richard Peace observed in the quote above, there is something about writing out a prayer that seems to make it more personal and real. Mark Harris observes that writing out prayers to the Lord has been of help to him in his seasons of dryness as well.[2] He especially likes to use the word *why* to begin his written prayers. In my case I let the prayer flow naturally from the notes I have made in my journal and try to focus it on some specific application of the text. Here are a few samples of such prayers from recent entries in my journal:

Lord, let all my teaching seek to establish myself and others firmly in Jesus.

O Lord, I would know You and the hope of my calling more and more each day.

O Lord, in Your mercy You sought me and saved me. Now I belong to You eternally. How sweet and how good is Your grace, O Lord!

Lord, give me the skills I need to serve You in the calling You have appointed to me. And let me trust You daily for all my needs. Keep me from idols, O Lord.

Lord, help me ever to be laboring for You. Give me strength, wisdom, and daily guidance that my faith may not be in vain.

Lord, let the trials that come to us have their positive effects. Let us welcome them as ways of knowing the presence of Jesus more fully in each of our lives.

What possible benefit could such short, summary prayers have for intensifying my time with the Lord in this spiritual discipline?

First, they draw the teaching of Scripture to a sharp focus and conclusion, leading me to present my study of God's Word back to him as an offering of prayer and firming up my understanding of what the passage I have been studying requires of me. In other words, they bring closure to my morning devotions, providing a concise summary of what I believe the Spirit of God has shown me and pointing me ahead to the day to come, leading me to consider how I might go forth and live more fully for Christ.

Second, they serve as a constant reminder and a helpful handle for brief prayer throughout the day. As my diary is always open before me, I cannot help but encounter these brief prayers again and again. When I do, I offer them back to the Lord, thus calling to mind again his message for me that day and restating my conclusions so that I will be more likely to keep the teaching of the text before me throughout the day.

This simple practice is an extremely important time of my morning prayers. I have often benefited at other times during the day by reflecting again on those pithy statements of praise, thanksgiving, dedication and reflection on the Lord's message for my life.

*Praying the psalms.* A second way of intensifying your time in prayer is to pray the psalms. Nothing has brought more vigor, satisfaction and consistency to my own prayers as this single discipline. There are a number of ways of approaching this discipline. Ronald Quillo in his book *The Psalms: Prayers of Many Moods* provides a list of the psalms for prayer according to the traditional hours of prayer—those set times of prayer throughout the day mentioned in chapter seven.[3] Eugene Peterson, on the other hand, recommends that we

> simply enter the sequence of the psalms as they are given to us in the
> Psalms, go from one to the next, one day to the next, taking what comes,
> learning to enter into what comes, whatever, practicing a sense of the pres-
> ence of God, deepening that awareness into colloquy with God.[4]

In other words, pray one psalm a day, taking them *seriatim* from the
psalter.

However you approach this effort to intensify your time in prayer,
you will need some practice. Not all of the psalms are in the form of
prayers, after all, and many of them will challenge you as you learn
how to make them your own in prayer. Some of the psalms you will be
able to pray verbatim, just as they are written. Others you will need to
translate into your own prayers by paraphrasing or praying respon-
sively a strophe (paragraph) at a time. In using the psalms in prayer,
you will want to adjust to a second person context—from speaking
about God to speaking to him. You will find that praying the psalms
will broaden your prayers, bring more focus and emotion to them, and
expand your understanding of God and his sovereign grace. The saints
of both the Old and New Testaments were so familiar with the
psalms—perhaps from a disciplined, daily use of them—that when
push came to shove in their lives and they needed prayers to bring their
urgent requests to the Lord, the psalms came readily to mind.[5] Praying
the psalms on a regular basis can greatly enrich your own practice of
the discipline of prayer and equip you for more powerful prayer at
other times as well.

Steven Wright has captured the rationale for and benefit from praying
the psalms well in his poem "Borrowed Words":[6]

> It is a justifiable theft
> This praying of borrowed words.
> My own words gave out years ago
> Like the wind when a ship hits the doldrums.
> I drifted
> Prayerless
> Until I learned how to borrow words.
> Now the pleas of Heman and Solomon
> The plaints of Asaph and David

Propel me on
As they leap from my lips
Heavenward,
Carried by Christ.

They were his words at first,
Borrowed by psalmists
And borrowed back when
Hanging on the cross he cried,
*My God, My God, why hast Thou forsaken me?*
Surely, my God,
Thou wilt not forsake me
If I borrow Thy words
And offer them back to Thee.

*Singing in prayer.* A third way of intensifying your use of the discipline of prayer derives from this, and that is to let the words of the psalms guide your posture and voice as you pray, even to the point of singing your prayers to the Lord. The psalms call us to raise our hands, lift up our voices, cry out to God, bow, kneel, shout, sing and various other activities in prayer. If your prayers have become flat, such exercises may be a way of beginning to return your prayer routine to a true discipline. Here I want to say just a word about singing as part of your time in prayer.

Whether you have a good singing voice or not, singing in prayer can greatly enhance your sense of meeting with the Lord. Calvin[7] wrote that singing can "incite us to pray to God and to praise him, and to meditate upon his works in order to love, fear, honor, and glorify him."[8] In singing we have the benefit both of the rich words of Spirit-filled men and women from many eras, as well as the moving melodies accompanying those words. Singing can reach to the heart as well as the mind, enlarging our vision of the life of faith, drawing us closer to the Lord in our prayers and increasing our love for him. Singing in prayer may require you to have a hymnal at hand. A hymnal can be a rich resource for bringing more heartfelt praise and thanks to God in your prayers. (It is not insignificant that the first book printed in America was *The Massachusetts Bay Psalm Book.*) A psalter, in which all the psalms are put to music for singing, is another useful tool, especially one that uses familiar hymns for its settings of the psalms, such as the *Trinity Psalter.*[9]

Great saints of God have made singing an important part of their devotional lives, as is evident from their familiarity with a great many hymns. On several occasions I had the pleasure of worshiping with James Montgomery Boice, and in all the times we worshiped together, I never saw him open a hymnal. Yet he knew every stanza of all the hymns we sang, and he sang them with evident passion and delight.[10] It may well have been that singing his prayers to the Lord was an important part of this great saint's practice of the disciplines of grace. Singing can help to bring new vitality to our own prayers as well.

### Intensifying the Discipline of Public Worship

Many Christians complain that services of worship leave them flat. In response to this, churches have attempted to enliven their services with bands and praise songs, dramatic vignettes or a much more casual liturgy overall. These changes may indeed help to bring more meaning and life into a service of worship. However, if the problem is in the worshiper and not the liturgy, then other means of recovering the discipline of public worship will have to be explored.

In my experience most Christians have very little idea about the purposes and content of worship. In our churches how to worship is more frequently caught than taught. We do what we do in worship by assimilating the practices of the church we choose to attend without often understanding why we do them. One way to recover the power of worship as a discipline of grace is to learn what worship is for, what each of its elements is designed to accomplish and why it is structured the way it is.

*Understanding the purpose of worship.* Worship is a congregation's corporate time for coming before the Lord to adore, praise and honor him through their songs, prayers, offerings and attentiveness to the Word of God. Worship, in other words, is for God, not us. We come together to please and serve him, not ourselves. Worshipers often complain that they didn't get anything out of a service, but getting something out of a service of worship is hardly the point. Putting ourselves into worship—heart, mind and strength—as expressions of our love for God is the point of worship. Worship is work, and we can only do this work in a way that will be pleasing to God and thoroughly enriching for us if we know what we are doing.

Worshipers—that is, all believers—therefore would do well to study the subject of worship, to understand better not only its biblical foundations and history but also its purpose, parts and procedures.[11] What is a call to worship? Why should a service begin with a hymn of praise? Is there a dialogical aspect to worship, and, if so, how do I enter into that dialogue? What is the role of preaching in worship? How can I learn to participate more intelligently and with greater personal benefit in all the various aspects of a service of worship? These are just a few of the questions that a study of worship might be able to answer, leaving us better equipped to enter worship as a special arena of the grace of God where we meet with him in an intensely personal way.

*Preparing for worship.* A second way to intensify your practice of worship is to prepare for worship well. Too often we come to church having rushed to get ready, bolted down some breakfast, glanced at the paper, and who knows what else. Once we get to church, we flit from place to place and person to person, dropping off kids, getting to Bible class or just looking for friends. Little time is given to settling our souls and preparing our hearts and minds for coming into the presence of God with his people.

Preparation for worship should begin at least on the evening prior to worship and should include some time in meditation and prayer, especially in searching your heart to make sure that no unconfessed sin is lurking there. Singing familiar hymns also helps focus your heart and mind on worship as you are getting ready for and driving to church. Before the service begins, a time of prolonged silence, waiting on the Lord and seeking communion with him, is a much better use of time than milling about in the sanctuary or auditorium chatting with friends. Study the order of service, if a printed one is provided. Preview the words to the hymns that you will be singing to make sure you have a good understanding of each stanza. Read over any texts of Scripture that are provided. Use the time prior to worship to set your heart on the business at hand, and you will find your practice of worship will be richer and more meaningful.

*Worship throughout the week.* Third, bring to the worship of God a rich bouquet of praises that you have gathered for him from the previous week. Throughout the week pay careful attention to all that God does for you: how he provides for you and your family, helps you in your work, blesses you in some relationship, gives you opportunities for serving him, shows you his glory in the created world or gives you a special experience of joy and delight. Note them in your journal. Then bring these praises with you to church and recall them as you participate in worship, thinking of them often during the course of the service, relating them to the prayers and hymns and the offerings of your fellow church members.

In other words, carry into worship the daily praises of your heart and lay them at the foot of the cross to celebrate the goodness of God, not just for those few moments of public worship but as the culmination of your week with the Lord. Doing so not only makes your time in public worship a richer and more personal experience, but it also creates an anticipation of worship in your soul throughout the week as you go about gathering the praises that you will bring to the Lord on his day.

### Intensifying the Discipline of Meditation

While not strictly a discipline in and of itself, meditation can be practiced as part of all the disciplines of grace. In meditation we allow our minds to settle into a zone where we are more acutely focused on a few words or ideas for a prolonged period of time, turning them over and over in our minds as we allow the Spirit of God to illuminate us in new and often surprising ways. Everything else gets blocked out or at least minimized as we concentrate on the words or idea turning over and over in our brain. The benefits of frequent meditation are so widely understood that I hardly need to say anything more here. I have already mentioned several practices in connection with the disciplines of the Word, prayer and worship that can greatly enhance your practice of meditation with greater power and effect. In the next chapter I suggest some ways of using meditation during times of solitude with the Lord.

Here, at the risk of sounding like a complete egghead throwback, I want to say a few words about the use of Gregorian chant in meditation.

Chant is the oldest music in the church, dating back to the earliest centuries of Christianity, and probably has links with the even more ancient music of the Hebrew synagogue. Most chant is in Latin, but recordings can also be found in Greek, English, French, Russian, Coptic and Gaelic (my favorite) as well. Chant is not like contemporary tonal music. It has no beat, is typically monophonic (that is, it sings a single melody line), uses a bare minimum of lyrics and has a decidedly otherworldly sound to it, suggesting an aura of majesty and mystery to listeners from all walks of life. Chant is still in use among several communions of the Christian church today, and even some well-known hymns derive their melodies from ancient chants, hymns such as "Be Thou My Vision" and "Hallelujah! Praise Jehovah!"

I have found meditating with chant to be extremely helpful in deepening my sense of the presence of God in the practice of spiritual disciplines, especially the discipline of solitude or when I am disciplining my routines. By learning some of the easier melodies and words, studying their English translation and biblical derivation, and singing them before the Lord, I experience a heightened sense of the majesty and mercy of God and feel myself coming more richly into the communion of saints from most ancient times.

The place to begin in using chant in meditation is not, as you might imagine, by studying chant. That effort will most likely lead to frustration, as many of the terms and references employed in formal studies of chant can be off-putting. Instead, purchase a cassette or CD of chant and just begin listening. Make sure that the music you purchase includes printed copies of the actual lyrics and their English translation, as well as perhaps some introductory material about chant itself. The more you listen to chant, the more certain melodies will start to become familiar and delightful to you. Before long you will find that you can hum the melody along with the singers, and with a little more effort you'll be patching in the original lyrics as well, singing right along with the choir. By devoting some time to this, you should be able to learn three or four chants that you can make your own.

My practice is to sing along with the music rather than trust myself to be able to gain the maximum benefit of this precious treasure on my own, although I frequently sing chants unaccompanied. Whether in my car or at home, I have never failed to find singing a familiar chant to be an uplifting experience. I feel carried into the very presence of God, born aloft by this strange, exotic, wonderful music into an atmosphere that is completely unlike anything I experience at other times. I have sung the same chant over and over, sometimes for up to an hour, each time dwelling more deeply on the simple lyric and immersing myself more completely in the melody, or neume. My eyes filling with tears; my heart greatly lifted; I experience a sense of the presence of God growing stronger and stronger each time through.

Not long ago I spoke at a conference on the role of the arts in the life of the kingdom of God, and I played three recordings of one particular chant so that the audience could experience the endearing and mysterious quality of this music. Afterward several people remarked at how wondrously the chants had lifted their thoughts toward God and asked for the particular recordings I had used.

Perhaps I can better convey some sense of what it is like to sing a chant as part of the discipline of meditation through the following poem, based on my experience of singing the *Kyrie*, one of the oldest and simplest chants. The *Kyrie* has only the lyrics (in Greek) "Lord, have mercy; Christ, have mercy; Lord, have mercy." The chant is thus addressed to Christ (in the Greek, *Kyrie*, alternating with *Christe*, the vocative case) and pleads for his forgiveness and renewing grace (again, in the Greek, *eleison*):

*Kyrie*

Quietly, clearly, and glorious in majesty
mounts up the name of the Almighty Lord;
swelling, it rises to heavenly heights, as it
fills up the air and expands in the soul.

Firmly it dwells on the vocative, stretches it
out, to embellish it, savor it. Then
downward the neume leads us, down to the depths of our
being; there, searches us, lifts us again,

back to the realm of forgiveness and grace. Then, no
pausing to breathe and no sound to alert,
changing itself imperceptibly, hear how the
vocative blends, from address to request.
Mercy inseparably linked to divinity!
Grace to a penitent heart is conveyed!
Joy like a welcome elixir arises, as
slowing, we end in a whisper of peace.

So valuable has this practice proven in intensifying my practice of meditation that I have taken the time to study chant in greater depth so that I might understand more fully this wonderful blessing that God has given to his church. You may find the study of chant, even if only at a cursory level, helpful to your use of this gift as well.[12]

### Intensifying Through the Study of Spiritual Disciplines

As I have mentioned, it is not my purpose in this book to provide a thorough study or theology of the disciplines of grace. That work has been done much more profitably by others. Your practice of the spiritual disciplines can be greatly enhanced by studying some of the recent books that have dealt with this subject in detail. Here I would like to mention just three.

Mark Harris's *Companions for Your Spiritual Journey* is a good place to begin, both as an introduction to the variety of spiritual disciplines as well as some of their more renowned practitioners from the past. Harris, an InterVarsity staff member, gives a highly personal and historically based overview of the disciplined life, helping us to know what to expect on this journey and pointing out obstacles we will encounter along the way. His discussions and examples of such disciplines as prayer, solitude and the Word of God provide valuable insights into how we might intensify the practice of these disciplines.

Dallas Willard's *The Spirit of the Disciplines* is the best introduction to the various disciplines and their use that I have found. Dr. Willard is a professor of philosophy at the University of Southern California. His approach in introducing us to the wide range of spiritual disciplines and their use is to call us to be like Jesus, to ask, in effect, "What would Jesus do?" not only in any situation in life but in private times with God as well. If we want to be like Jesus in the tight squeezes and daily challenges of life, we need to be more like him in our practice of the disciplines of grace. Dr. Willard's book is an excellent introduction and overview of this field.

Finally, let me recommend the handbook edited by Richard J. Foster and James Bryan Smith, *Devotional Classics*. This book introduces us to the vast field of devotional literature from all the periods of church history, providing samples of the great devotional classics and leading the reader through devotional exercises designed to give more of the experience of what the various writers address. This is an excellent handbook for personal or group use and can be a rich resource for intensifying your experience in the disciplines of grace.

We must not be content with practicing mere spiritual routines. God has provided disciplines of grace for us. If our use of those disciplines has lost its cutting edge, then we must take steps to increase or intensify our involvement in these special arenas of grace until, exhausted but exhilarated from our wrestling with the Lord, we find the blessing that he intends for us from these intense and personal encounters with him in the presence of his Word and Spirit.

## Questions for Study or Discussion

1. Would you describe your practice of the spiritual disciplines as intense and personal? Why or why not?

2. Which of the suggestions for intensifying the time in spiritual disciplines most appeals to you? How could you adopt this for your own practice?

3. How will your schedule have to change as a result of beginning to intensify your practice of spiritual disciplines? What will you need to give up?

4. What obstacles to intensifying your practice of spiritual disciplines can you anticipate? What are some ways that you might prepare to overcome those obstacles?

5. What is the most important idea you have learned from this chapter? How will this help you in achieving the goals you set for this study?

# 9

## innovating disciplines

*When true religion falls under a general and remarkable decay, it is time for all that are concerned to awaken and rouse themselves to fresh vigor and activity, in their several posts of service . . . each of us should inquire, What can I do to strengthen the things which remain and are ready to die, as well as to recover what is lost?*
ISAAC WATTS

*And your sons and your daughters shall prophesy, your old men shall dream dreams, your young men shall see visions.*
JOEL 2:28

*M*arriage has been for me like Dorothy emerging from her black and white, tornado-tossed home into the glorious color and wonder of the Land of Oz. I never fail to be amazed at the grace that God shows me in the gift of my wife and in the many ways she has expanded and enriched my horizons on life. Not least of these is the fact that she has effected a culinary revolution in my diet.

In my childhood home I was the second of four large, always-hungry boys. My mom was a good cook, and we never lacked for ample portions. But I would not describe her as adventuresome in this regard. She had a set dinner menu that she repeated faithfully and diligently for all the years I lived at home: beef stew, pot roast, hot dogs, beans of various kinds, corn, fried chicken, mashed potatoes, hamburger, meat loaf and an occasional lasagna or pizza. We loved her cooking, and there were seldom any leftovers. For all we knew, this was what everybody ate for dinner on a regular basis. When I went to college, I took my meals at the athletic dining hall where, if anything, the cuisine was even more limited than what I had known at home (if it's Wednesday, it must be mystery meat).

And then Susie came along. A born-and-bred Southern girl, reared on the best of Dixie cuisine together with the tastes and recipes her Yankee mother had brought into her own marriage, Susie knew how to eat. Before we were married, I had managed well for twenty-one years, my palate completely unaware of its deprivation or of the wondrous foods that awaited it.

I remember one of the first meals Susie fixed for us after our honeymoon. We were still in school at the time. I came home from class to our little trailer on the outskirts of town, and as soon as I approached the front door, I could smell the glorious aromas mingling in the kitchen. When I came inside, the trailer was filled with strange, sweet, tantalizing smells. I greeted Susie, asked what was for dinner and being told "a surprise," relaxed on the couch to read the paper while I waited.

When I sat down at the table and saw what was spread before me, I felt a surge of fear and dread. "What's this?" I asked, then almost wished I hadn't. "Chicken livers and bacon, with black-eyed peas over rice and mustard greens." "Mmmm," I managed to say. I had heard about liver and how awful it was. In my family only my mother and grandmother ate liver, but, hey, they also ate brains and eggplant. I had harvested mustard greens on the farm where I worked while I was in high school, and I remember thinking then, *Man, who eats this stuff?* And black-eyed peas? Well, maybe the rice (with which I was familiar, although only ever with sugar and cinnamon, never beans) would cover the taste.

Needless to say, I was reluctant to dig in. But I had to admit, it smelled good, and from what I had heard, it would all be very good for me. I watched as Susie seasoned her plate, then carefully followed suit. I placed my napkin on my lap, took a drink of water, looked at Susie and smiled. Then I took a bite of the rice and black-eyed peas, which I considered the safest place to start. *Hmmm, that's pretty good*, I thought. Susie poured a little vinegar (vinegar?) on her mustard greens, so I did too. I took my first bite of greens, and they melted sumptuously in my mouth. I ate the whole helping without stopping, then returned to the peas and rice and nearly finished them off as well. But I studiously avoided the chicken livers as long as I could. Finally, however, the time came to screw up my courage and have a taste. I cut a piece of liver, added a half slice of bacon and put it in my mouth. The texture was new and strange but not in the least unpleasant. The bacon tempered and brightened the strong, earthy flavor of the liver, making it fairly dance on my palate. I chewed heartily, enjoying this new taste as fully as possible. I then ate the whole plateful and asked for more.

In our home library there are more cookbooks than commentaries, and during our thirty years of marriage I have gained more benefit from this than if it were the other way around. Almost every week some new recipe ends up on my plate, either from one of Susie's cookbooks or from her own imaginative mind, and I am enriched and delighted in new and altogether wonderful ways. I am also certain that not only have my taste buds been richly exercised and my palate generously blessed, but I am also a healthier man today than I would have been had I never been swept up in the culinary revolution that marriage to Susie has brought into my life. My diet had gone stale, was stuck in a rut, and I didn't even know it. But I have been liberated to new worlds of taste, texture, aroma and vitality by the dietary innovations Susie has brought into my life. Oh, we still enjoy beef stew and meat loaf, but now their goodness is enhanced and enriched by the relative infrequency with which they occur in our weekly menu, which is crowded with new favorites and the latest dietary innovations each week.

### Fear of Innovation

There is, in most of us, something of an in-built fear of new things. From the terror we experienced on our first day of school, to our dread of moving to a new city or changing to a new job, or the caution with which we enter into new relationships, people, being creatures of habit, are reluctant to change. We tend to seek comfort zones in life, familiar places where we know the terrain and feel safe and secure. This is what feels good to us, what has worked for us, and we will change those comfort zones only after a great deal of hemming and hawing and trying to talk ourselves out of it.

The same is true in our spiritual lives and, in particular, in our practice of the disciplines of grace. We have always done this, that or the other and never felt a need to add new disciplines to our walk with the Lord. These old, reliable practices have served us well, we suppose, and if it ain't broke, don't fix it.

But what if it is broke? What if we sense that our faith is falling into decay, even if it is not "general and remarkable," and those old disciplines are beginning to feel more like routines than the means of growth in grace that God intends them to be? At such times, as we have seen, it may be necessary to "strengthen the things that remain"—our existing disciplines—either by increasing our time in them or intensifying them in one way or another. Or it may be time to consider adding some new disciplines to our walk with the Lord, to recover what is lost in the disciplines of grace, perhaps because we have never taken the time to find them in the first place.

The disciplines of grace are like a toolbox for the life of faith. God has been pleased to place in this box a wondrous variety of tools for us to use in building the house of faith that is our lives in Christ. Many of us, however, use that toolbox like I use my actual toolbox whenever some home repair or maintenance is required: if it can't be repaired by a hammer or a screwdriver, then I hope it will just go away, or I call in someone else to fix it. I may see a wide array of tools in that box, one or more of which might make my work easier and save me some money, but I would have to learn how to use that tool first, and that means innovation, and I am a reluctant innovator when it comes to tools, as with almost everything else.

The disciplines of grace are the tools of home improvement for the life of faith. At one time or another every one of them will be necessary for our growth and well-being in the Lord. If it were not so, the Lord would not have placed them there for us. If all we ever use are the hammers and screwdrivers in our toolbox—the Word, prayer and worship—we will find that our house of faith will often fall into decay and disrepair of the sort that these tools are not adequate in and of themselves to fix. We need to familiarize ourselves with all the tools at our disposal, gaining enough mastery of each of them that we can use them with confidence and benefit for our walk with the Lord.

And for most of us, alas, that will mean innovation—adding new disciplines to our practice.

In order to help us gain some familiarity with these tools, I will introduce in this chapter two disciplines that are neglected by the vast majority of believers. I will then suggest some ways of making them part of our regular practice of the disciplines of grace.

## The Discipline of Fasting

Very few Christians practice any other fast than the one they routinely break in the morning when they awake. Yet, as we saw earlier, the Lord expects his followers to practice the discipline of fasting as a means of grace and growth. The early Christians were encouraged to fast two days a week, one to recall the Lord's betrayal (Wednesday) and one his suffering (Friday).[1] Abraham Kuyper defined fasting as "a temporary abstaining from customary food or drink, for devotional reasons."[2] I want to emphasize that last prepositional phrase: "for devotional reasons." That is, merely going without food or drink for an extended period of time has no particular value in and of itself. Rather, it falls into the category of *opera operata*. Our fasting must have a devotional focus; that is, it must find us drawing aside from these familiar activities in order to concentrate our focus more exclusively on the Lord and his will for our lives (Is 58:1-12). As Kuyper notes, fasting enables us to discipline our bodies[3]— and everything in which they are involved—in order to increase devotion to the Lord in the whole of life:

> For it is the body that protests when we would fast. It is the body that occupies almost all of our time, demanding to be fed and clothed and tended. We are so busy from morning till night fulfilling the demands of the body, that there is barely a half hour left in the day for quiet meditation. That is a common complaint.
>
> Paul says, "I buffet my body to bring it into bondage." Thereby he reverses the natural tendency which says, "My body is master and I am its servant."[4]

According to Scripture, fasting can be entered into for a number of excellent reasons.

*Fasting for repentance.* First, we may fast when we sense a need for repentance from some sin, whether in ourselves, in others or in the church as a whole. The people of Nineveh devoted themselves to fasting in order to gain and demonstrate repentance for the sins for which they had fallen under the judgment of God (Jon 3). Daniel, on the other hand, fasted for the sins of Israel, with which he identified but from which he seems to have been free of guilt (Dan 9). If we are struggling with some sin, or if someone we know is, or if we have a sense that our church or the church as a whole needs to come to repentance for sin, fasting is an excellent discipline for seeking the Lord concerning this grace.

*Fasting as preparation for growth.* According to Zechariah 8:18-22, fasting can be excellent preparation for an anticipated season of church growth. If your church is building a new facility, for example, experts tell us that you might expect as much as a 30 percent increase in attendance the first week. It may be wise for the congregation to enter on a season of fasting so that this new phase in your church's life can be one of "joy and gladness, and cheerful feasts" and that "there shall come people, and the inhabitants of many cities." Seeking God's grace and wisdom in a season of fasting may help to make this new phase of your congregation's life a time of genuine renewal. Or if your church is planning a special outreach activity—a series of meetings, vacation Bible school or a special retreat, for example—fasting in anticipation of the Lord's blessing may well help to secure his blessings for the effort.

In a similar way, fasting to concentrate on some area of personal growth in the Lord may be beneficial. For example, as I have mentioned, each year I like to review my personal mission statement and the goals and objectives I have set for my life. Then I consider areas in which I need to grow and life goals for the coming year. In preparation for this I have found that a time of fasting can wondrously compose and focus my mind and spirit on this important task, helping me to seek the Lord's will for the coming year.

*Fasting as a memorial.* According to Esther 9:29-32, fasting is an excellent way of memorializing important events in the life of our church or our own lives. It can help us to relive the grace of God extended to us during that period and deepen our love for him in profound and lasting ways.

Similarly, fasting is appropriate to commemorate tragic events in the lives of those we love or the community of faith (1 Sam 31:11-13). At such times fasting reminds us of the frailty of our flesh and of our need for the Lord's sustaining grace in all we do.

*Fasting for enemies.* In Psalm 35:13-14 the psalmist reports that he fasted for his enemies—that the grace of God might overwhelm and change them. We may not know many adversaries to our faith in this country—although they certainly exist—but our brothers and sisters in other lands are constantly under assault by enemies of the faith. Our fasts for those enemies could see many of them coming to conviction of sin and repentance to new life in Christ, bringing relief and renewal to the members of Christ's body in those lands (Ps 83:16).

*Fasting to know God's will.* Fasting can also be beneficial at times when we seek to know the will of the Lord more deeply from the Word of God (Ex 34:27-28), such as during a retreat or conference, or when we have set aside special time for study or preparation to teach.

*Fasting for new ministries.* We may also fast in an intercessory way for others who are entering into a new or even potentially dangerous endeavor (Esther 4:1-3), such as when missionaries are being commissioned. In the same way, fasting as preparation for new ministry undertakings is supported by both the Old and New Testaments (Ezra 8:21-23; Acts 13:2-3). Fasting can also be an important tool for preparing us to do battle with the devil—to guard and fortify us in the face of temptation or support us through times of trial or deprivation (Mt 4:1-11).

What Kuyper noted a hundred years ago is still true today:

> Unhesitatingly we recommend fasting for the Christians of today. In fact, we are inclined to say that there is more reason for fasting in our day than ever before. Corrupted human nature yearns for luxury, and tends to become more corrupt as wealth and luxury increase. God knows that we cannot well be checked except by burdens and sorrows. And he himself has suggested fasting, by means of which we may guard against the unspiritual influence of ease and luxury.[5]

But how do we fast? For how long? And how may we prepare ourselves for fasting, so that we can gain the most benefit from this important spiritual discipline?

*Guidelines for fasting.* Jesus set forth the guidelines for fasting in Matthew 6:16-18. First, we are not to make a public show of our fasting, either by contrived displays of suffering or brash boasts of self-denial (Lk 18:12). We are to keep up our normal demeanor and routine as far as possible, making every effort to conceal the fact that we have set aside this time for a special season of devotion. Second, we are to fast unto the

Lord. This suggests that our fast should have some specific purpose or object, perhaps one of those I indicated above. We declare to the Lord our purpose for entering into a season of fasting, and then we revisit that purpose frequently during the fast, as our body (so helpful during such times) reminds us that it is under discipline for devotion's sake.

As for how long we fast, that strikes me as being completely subjective. God can guide you in this matter, especially if fasting is a new discipline for you. I would suggest that you begin by fasting one meal for a day—perhaps lunch. Use that time instead to concentrate on the object of your fast in prayer, meditate, search the Scripture or talk with a soul friend. If the last is your preferred occupation for fasting, be sure to leave time for prayer before you leave. Fasting one day a month or once a week can also be beneficial. In such cases I recommend fasting from dinner of the previous night to dinner the night of your fast. That way you don't end up sitting at the dinner table with your family showing them how spiritual you are. More extended fasts are also possible, but I would suggest consulting other literature and perhaps even your physician before undertaking such a trial of your faith.

*Preparing for a fast.* It is important to prepare for your season of fast as well. Think carefully about the purpose. Be sure you know the names of those for whom you want to pray or the details of the situation you are commemorating or for which you are planning to intercede. Write out some Scripture to use during your fast, both to help you focus on the object of your fast and to keep your body in subjection when its growling and complaining tempts you to abandon your discipline. You might tell your stomach, for example, "I have meat to eat that ye know not of" (Jn 4:32), or "I have esteemed the words of his mouth more than my necessary *food*" (Job 23:12). You might tell your parched throat, "As a deer longs for flowing streams, / so my soul longs for you, O God" (Ps 42:1 NRSV). Careful preparation for a fast can help to make your practice of this discipline more meaningful and satisfying as a means of encountering the Lord for the purpose you have determined and of knowing his powerful, transforming work in your life.

We do not fast because we are creatures of habit, and one of our habits occurs three times a day, right on schedule. Yet we may begin to discipline our bodies—and all the activities in which they are involved—and to develop new habits by entering into the practice of fasting to the Lord as a new discipline from our toolbox of faith. And you may find that adding this new discipline to your repertoire will revitalize all your practice in these special arenas of grace, helping you to move from routine to renewal in your practice of the disciplines of grace.

### The Discipline of Solitude with the Lord

If our generation of Christians has been negligent in the discipline of fasting, the discipline of solitude with the Lord is all but unknown among us. We are an activist people, squeezed into the mold of our activist contemporaries, and we have almost no time for being alone and little inclination toward it. Yet solitude, especially solitude with the Lord, is a most valuable, most important practice for us to recover. As Dallas Willard describes this discipline:

> In solitude, we purposefully abstain from interaction with other human beings, denying ourselves companionship and all that comes from our conscious interaction with others. We close ourselves away; we go to the ocean, to the desert, the wilderness, or to the anonymity of the urban crowd. This is not just rest or refreshment from nature, though that too can contribute to our spiritual well-being. Solitude is choosing to be *alone* and to dwell on our experience of isolation from other human beings.[6]

*Solitude requires time.* In my experience three factors make for an effective time of solitude with the Lord. The first is time. Solitude with the Lord requires time, which can only be garnered by setting aside some of the other activities that consume our lives on a regular basis. It does not have to be a lot of time either. We can benefit from being alone in the Lord's presence for as little as fifteen or twenty minutes, while we are much more likely to encounter him in a more intense and personal way if we have up to an hour or more. Such blocks of time in our schedules do not arise spontaneously; we do not find that suddenly we have an empty thirty or forty minutes so why not withdraw for a time of solitude with the Lord? Rather, we will need to capture that time, to plan for it and guard it carefully lest it become gobbled up by some lesser demand.

*Solitude requires a special place.* Second, solitude with the Lord requires a place where we can be free from distractions or interruptions. Willard mentions the ocean, desert or wilderness as possible venues for solitude.

Unhappily, not everyone will have ready access to one of these, in which case a park, stream or even one's own backyard might do just as well. But Willard also mentions "the anonymity of the urban crowd" as a likely place to know solitude with the Lord. The key here is "anonymity." I agree with Willard that a cafe, library or museum can be an excellent venue for meeting alone with the Lord as long as you can avoid encounters with people who know you and who may unwittingly steal the time you have set aside. Some of the richest times of solitude with the Lord that I have known have been at a local restaurant or in a crowded cafe. Obviously, the venue is not so important. Preserving the time in that venue for devotion to the Lord is what matters.

*Solitude requires a focus.* Third, an effective time of solitude with the Lord requires some focus for entering into his presence. Scripture, prayer, your devotional journal or a hymnal can provide such a focus. Even recordings of meditative hymns, chants or inspirational music from the great masters can serve to focus our attention on the Lord during a season of solitude. Works of art in a museum or a book of poems can also fulfill this purpose. In my case what usually happens is that several things come into play to help focus my attention on the Lord, draw me into his presence and reveal his glory in some new and exciting way. I may be reading a poem of Czeslaw Milosz, for example, on the sufferings of the people of Warsaw during the war and be reminded of the sufferings of our Lord Jesus on the cross as they are recorded in Psalms 22 and 69. This leads me to sing something like "O Sacred Head Now Wounded" or to praise him for the grace he has shown a sinner such as I. Or I may be studying a painting by Andrew Wyeth, marveling at the detail of his representation and soaking up the beauty of the whole, and be reminded that all such gifts come to us from God, who provides even for those who do not know him (Ps 68:18), so that we might be blessed by his greatness and grace from all directions all day long. This again will lead to my giving him praise and thanks for all his goodness.

Here is how one of my students, Jean-Marie VunCannon, describes her own practice of solitude:

> For several years I have had a standing "coffee date" with the Lord. On Fridays, after taking my child to school, I head to my favorite coffee shop (aptly named "Holy Grounds"). I use the time primarily for journaling, which takes the form of an ongoing letter to God. I take my Bible with me,

because often in the course of journaling, God brings to mind a passage that encourages me, addresses a certain need, or exposes a hidden sin. Often I begin by reading past entries, and am amazed to see how God has answered prayers and guided me through difficult times. Sometimes I see that God has answered a prayer that I had forgotten I had prayed.[7]

For me one of the most effective means of meeting with God and focusing on his glory during a season of solitude is to be alone with him amid the beauty of his creation. I have been encouraged in this approach to practicing the discipline of solitude by the example of the ancient Celtic Christians, who seem to have had a special ability to see the Lord in the details of the natural world. According to Philip Sheldrake, "The Celtic Christian attitude to nature involved a profound sense of the immanence of God. . . . Nature was a kind of second sacred book, parallel to the scriptures, that revealed the divine."[8] We can see this very clearly in the following excerpts from a poem from the Celtic period (ca. A.D. 450-1000):

I have a hut in the wood, none knows it but my Lord; an ash tree this side, a hazel on the other, a great tree on a mound encloses it. . . .

The size of my hut, small yet not small, a place of familiar paths; the she-bird in its dress of blackbird colour sings a melodious strain from its gable.
. . .

Excellent fresh springs—a cup of water, splendid to drink—they gush forth abundantly; yew berries, bird-cherries. . . .

Peaceful, in crowds, a grave host of the countryside, an assembly at my house; foxes come to the wood before it—it is delightful. . . .

A beautiful pine makes music to me, it is not hired; through Christ I fare no worse at any time than you do.

Though you delight in your own enjoyments, greater than all wealth, for my part I am grateful for what is given me from my dear Christ.

Without an hour of quarrel, without the noise of strife which disturbs you, grateful to the Prince who gives every good to me in my hut.[9]

For the Celtic Christians certain places were regarded as *thin places*, where the membrane that separates the spiritual and the natural worlds was especially fine, so that a person's sense of being in the presence of

God and other spiritual beings was greatly enhanced. This is what we should expect from the created world, which is constantly proclaiming the glory and the majesty of the Lord (Ps 8:1; 19:1-6). The created world reveals the goodness of God—his immensity, grandeur, power, beauty, wisdom and splendor—and can thus be a rich source for us as we seek to meet with the Lord in a time of solitude.

From my front porch I look out across rich pastures to Laurel Mountain, a ten-mile long, tree-covered prominence that is part of the Appalachian chain. Deep woods recede to the southwest, and a copse of poplars protects our home from north winds at the back. These woods are home to over forty different kinds of birds who routinely visit our feeders or drift through the air space over our yard displaying their many-colored vestments and filling the air with distinct and beautiful songs. I have found retreating to my front porch for a season of solitude with the Lord to be among the most important times of my week. There I can look out on Laurel Mountain and recall the psalmist's declaration of how the mountains were formed by the power of almighty God (Ps 104:5-9). I watch the trees waving in the breeze and imagine them clapping their hands for joy in anticipation of the Lord's coming (Ps 96:11-13). I hear and see the many different birds and am overwhelmed by the intricacy, variety and beauty of the creation, and him who is responsible for it all (Gen 1).

Sometimes during my revelries alone with the Lord the presence of man will intrude—a shotgun report off in the woods, an automobile down the road, a phone call, a passing airplane. However, even these can, at such times, serve to enhance my sense of the Lord's goodness, leading me to think about the dignity of work, the wonder of man's creative genius or the importance of friends and family. As I focus on the beauty around me, I often gain new insights into God's goodness in my own life, his providential care for his people, his mighty sovereign power or his constant presence with us. From time to time I record my reflections in my journal or in a poem, which then serves as a helpful reminder and review that I can visit over and over again, and can even result in my reaching out to others in the love of Christ.

On one such occasion I sat alone with the Lord on a very cold February morning. The sky was gray, and snow was threatening. The wind was still, and every sound was heightened. On that morning loggers

were at work off in a neighbor's woods. I could hear their chain saws rip-
ping through the poplar trees, the tractor dragging the logs and lining
them up for the logging trucks that would carry them away. None of this
was visible to me, but I could see it all, and I was led to give praise and
thanks to God for men and women who work with their hands amid the
harsh elements so that I might enjoy the comforts of home, hearth, safe
travel and so forth.

The sound of their activities echoed all around. Suddenly I was
reminded of a neighbor, Mrs. Shaw, whose youngest son, Tommy, had
been killed in a logging accident the previous September. Her little
bookshop is just west of our home across a low ridge. I knew that she
could hear the sounds of logging too. I wondered what sad thoughts
those sounds brought to her mind, and how she must have held on to
the Lord as she coped with her grief. I began to pray for her and her
family that the Lord might comfort them with his presence and remind
them of his promise that all things work together for good for those
who, like Mrs. Shaw, love him and have been called according to his
purpose. A poem began to take shape in my mind, which ultimately
turned out as follows.

*Logging*
For Mrs. Shaw,
thinking of you, and remembering Tommy


The nearby woods resound this morning with
the sounds of unseen loggers. Chain saws chew
their way through brittle bark and pulp-bound pith.

A tractor growls and groans as it drags the new
logs out and lays them side by side upon
a ridge, where crab-clawed crane arms hoist the queue

onto rumbling trucks which, loaded, soon are gone
to local lumberyards. The shouts and calls
of hidden lumberjacks echo upon
the air to warn as yet more timber falls
with cracks and crashings to the frozen ground.
This rustic chorus penetrates the walls

of every home and shop for miles around.
In one of these, intruding like a thief
who steals a youngest child, the haunting sound

accosts a mother, who clings to her belief
in God, and logs another day of grief.

Some months later, at Susie's recommendation, I was able to give a copy of this poem to Mrs. Shaw, who received it with tears of gratitude and joy.

As Philip Sheldrake says of the Celtic Christian experience of nature:

There was no real divide between this world and the "other" world of divine and spiritual beings. God was close at hand, but so were the saints and the angels. The nearness of God to creation went hand in hand with a sense of the heavenly powers surrounding people day and night.[10]

Meeting with God in times of solitude can be greatly enhanced by retreating into the natural world to contemplate him in all his goodness and glory. Our encounters there can deepen our relationship with him, enabling us to grow in grace and equipping us to serve others in his name.

### Getting Started in Fasting and Solitude

It must have seemed strange to those who heard and read the prophesy of Joel prior to the time of the apostles, to think that ordinary folk might be given prophetic gifts and entrusted with the message of God's grace. In fact, we know this was a strange, new idea, for, when it actually came to pass on that Day of Pentecost in Acts 2, people were confused and curious about what they were seeing and hearing. How could it be that ordinary Jews from all places on the earth were going about like prophets, proclaiming the greatness of the Lord?

Similarly, it may seem strange to think of ourselves as regularly practicing such disciplines as fasting and solitude with the Lord. Perhaps we have only thought of these as disciplines for the "really spiritual" followers of Christ, like monks in the desert, full-time ascetics or big-name Christian leaders. We have a hard time imagining that our own practice of the disciplines of grace might include such activities on a regular basis.

But just as the Spirit of God brought that first generation of believers into a revolution of bearing witness to the Lord, so he brought them, and us with them, into a revolution of disciplines. He has given us a glorious toolbox for building our own house of faith in the Lord. From time to time that house of faith will be in need of repair. Or we'll want to add a new room on in order to keep up with the growth we are experiencing or expecting. The familiar tools with which we have been working don't seem to be getting the job done, or they are proving inadequate to the task at hand. Something more seems to be needed so that we might recover the joy and thrill of being with the Lord in those special arenas of grace and continue building our house.

At such times, when our spiritual palate has gone flat and everything tastes the same in our walk with the Lord—when our disciplines are little more than mere routines, and we are neither glorying in the Lord nor growing in his grace—putting some new food on the table may be just the solution we need. And it may be that fasting and solitude with the Lord would be good places to begin.

*Set realistic goals.* But begin small. Set realistic goals for your use of these disciplines and don't bite off more than you can chew of this part of the Lord's menu until you have acquired a taste for them. Otherwise, their tastes and textures may offend you, you may become discouraged by the difficulty of practicing these disciplines, and it may be a long time before you will return to them again.

*Have a clear focus.* What will be the purpose of your fast? For whom or what will you be praying and fasting before the Lord? To what end? What will serve to focus your attention on the Lord as you enter into a season of solitude with him? If your answer is "anything and everything," your experience is most likely to be "nothing at all." Choose carefully the guide that is to lead you during your time of solitude and concentrate your efforts on seeing the glory of God through it.

*Prepare well.* Be careful to prepare for these disciplines as well. Have Scripture ready to sustain you for your fast. Know the people and facts concerning your purpose. Prepare yourself to resist every temptation that seeks to draw you out of this discipline by appealing to the needs of your flesh. Similarly, make certain that you have chosen a proper place and are familiar with your chosen guide for your time of solitude. It does no good to choose the museum for your morning of solitude with the Lord if it's not open that day or if you have no idea about what aspects of its collection might be most conducive to your purposes in seeking time alone with the Lord. Prepare well for the practice of these disciplines, and you will be more thoroughly rewarded in them.

*Prepare for battle.* Finally, remember that like all the disciplines of grace, fasting and solitude are hard work. We have discussed the disciplines in fairly mild terms thus far, but in reality the disciplines of grace are the no man's land of the life of faith, where enemy fire rages from every angle, seeking to destroy and defeat us in our walk with the Lord. We have all experienced this in our times of reading God's Word and praying—how easily our minds wander or we drift off to sleep or how often we come out of such times with nothing to show for them. This will be more so as we enter into those extended periods of spiritual discipline such as fasting and solitude require. Be prepared to do fierce battle with the enemy of our souls, who will give his all to discourage you and keep you from benefiting from the time and effort you invest in these disciplines. Resist him, and he will flee the field, but be prepared to struggle mightily against him as he turns all his fire against you to drive you off this special terrain. Any attempt to innovate spiritual disciplines in our walk with the Lord is a special affront to the devil, like opening up a new battlefront in our warfare against him. He will rush to defend it and seek with all his might to drive you back to your safe enclosure once again.

But stand firm. Prepare well, focus clearly and persevere by faith. Expect the Spirit of God and his angelic hosts to come to your aid as surely as he did to the Lord (Ps 91:11-12; Mt 4). The victory is ours, and the disciplines of grace are both the training ground where we learn to deploy the weapons of our warfare with greater ability, as well as the latest front in our assault against the kingdom of darkness. The more of them we master and deploy, the sooner will come our victories over the enemy of our souls.

## Questions for Study or Discussion

1. Have you ever fasted for any length of time? If not, what has prevented you? If so, describe your experience.

2. What might be a good place for you to seek solitude with the Lord? Why? What might serve as your focus for such a time?

3. What will have to change in your normal routines for you to innovate new disciplines? How can you prepare for this?

4. Review the disciplines introduced in chapter two. Which of these would you like to see more of in your life? How do you think they would benefit you?

5. What is the most important lesson you have learned from this chapter? How might it help you realize the goals you have established for this study?

# 10

# finding a soul friend

*Today all the really vital questions that touch the depths of existence enter
man's consciousness through the medium of persons in whom
these questions are, as it were, incarnated.*
HELMUT THIELICKE

*And let us consider how to provoke one another to love and good deeds.*
HEBREWS 10:24 (NRSV)

*A* wonderful vignette from the life of Brendan (ca. 489-570),
who would later be renowned as "The Navigator," illustrates the important role that others can play in helping us to gain the most from the disciplines of grace.

As a child Brendan was fostered (apprenticed) to Bishop Erc, a
saintly pastor who took responsibility to help him begin mastering the
disciplines of grace and learning the Scriptures. Brendan used to accom-
pany his mentor on preaching tours, where he had opportunity to see in
this godly man's life the outworking of those disciplines of grace that he
was expected to master.

On one occasion Brendan was traveling with Bishop Erc as he went
out into the countryside to preach in a small community. Brendan
remained behind in the chariot and was working at reciting his psalms.
His concentration was so intense that he did not notice a little girl about
his own age who had come up to the chariot and was trying to enter it,
hoping to play with Brendan. When suddenly he became aware of her,

he cursed at her and struck her with the reins, ordering her to go away and leave him alone.

Not a good idea, as it turned out, since this was the young daughter of the local king (ever have a day like that?). When Bishop Erc discovered what Brendan had done, he was shocked and scolded him mightily. Humbled and disgraced, Brendan asked to be assigned some act of penance, whereby he might demonstrate sorrow for his sin and show the Lord and the local people that he was earnest about wanting to make things right.[1] The bishop directed him to spend the night in a nearby cave, seeking grace and renewal from the Lord. Brendan readily complied and entered the cave about nightfall. Unknown to him, Bishop Erc remained outside the cave all night praying for his young charge and standing ready to come to his assistance if he should become frightened. All night long Brendan sang his psalms of praise to the Lord in such passionate and beautiful tones that the glorious music carried for miles around and ministered the grace of God to Bishop Erc and many in the local community. In the morning, when Brendan emerged from the cave, both his mentor and he had been renewed by their prayers and the grace of God at work through each of them.[2]

**The Soul Friend**

This story illustrates the Celtic Christian idea of the *anamcara* or "soul friend." It was the practice of church leaders during the period of the Celtic Revival (ca. A.D. 430-790)[3] to bind themselves to one another for the sake of mutual encouragement and support in growth and service to the Lord. Esther De Waal summarizes the work of the *anamcara* as follows:

> It is the soul-friend who helps above all, who brings medicine for the soul, who supports and who challenges throughout one's life. . . . The soul-friend was the spiritual guide who helped everyone find his or her own path. . . . [Soul-friendship] was true friendship, with warmth and intimacy and honesty, and there is a profound respect for the other's wisdom, despite age or gender differences, as the source of blessing. But it was not merely affirmative. This is, much more than what so often the modern reduction has made of it, finding someone to "share the journey—walk the path." There is challenge as well, confrontation, not collusion.[4]

The practice of soul friendship was not limited to individuals alone.

Often a Celtic saint—like Brendan—would have two or more soul friends to depend upon in different ways. Or a group of thirteen missionary-monks—a team leader and twelve associates—would serve as soul friends together as they embarked on some new mission to take the gospel to the lost, as when Columbanus sailed from Ireland to Gaul late in the sixth century. The power that this relationship afforded to sustain spiritual strength, vision for mission and physical endurance against often incredible odds may well be one of the reasons that the Celtic Revival enjoyed such astonishing success in spreading the gospel and civilizing pagan lands for nearly three hundred fifty years.

The support and encouragement of soul friends can be critical to helping us succeed during those times when our spiritual disciplines droop or we seek to rebuild those disciplines through increasing the time allotted for them, intensifying our involvement with them or taking on new disciplines for the first time. The friendship, guidance, example and accountability that such a relationship provides can help us get beyond mere spiritual routines into the glory and transformation that practicing the disciplines of grace are meant to provide. It also provides a context for encouraging one another in love to God and for showing his love to others. A relationship with a soul friend is not like mentoring, although it may begin that way; rather, there is give-and-take, a mutual dependency that occurs in such a relationship that finds both parties benefiting in their walk with the Lord. Soul friends can become vital, ongoing collaborators in helping us to grow in grace and service to the Lord.

### Soul Friends in Scripture and History

It does not surprise us to see examples of this relationship taught and illustrated in the Scripture. Solomon tells us, "Iron sharpens iron, / and one person sharpens the wits of another" (Prov 27:17 NRSV). The writer of Hebrews urged his readers to consider carefully how they might serve one another in growth and ministry (Heb 10:24). Moses and Jethro demonstrated the mutual benefit this kind of relationship can bring. Jethro gave practical advice to Moses at a crucial junction in his ministry, and Moses helped Jethro turn from paganism to serve the living and true God. David and Jonathan, Daniel and his three friends, and Barnabas and Paul seem to have enjoyed this kind of relationship as well. The work of our Lord Jesus in preparing his disciples for leadership clearly demonstrates the power of such relationships for encouraging growth and helping to prepare God's people for ministry in his name.[5]

The New Testament contains many instructions and exhortations concerning our responsibility to help one another in the walk of faith. We are to love and pray for one another, bear one another's burdens, rebuke and admonish one another, teach one another, care for one another, serve one another with spiritual gifts, and stimulate one another to love and good works. Relationships of mutual encouragement and support are integral to a healthy walk with the Lord. We should therefore expect that they would be valuable aids in helping us move from routine to renewal in the practice of spiritual disciplines.

In addition to the Celtic period, church history shows us many examples of soul friends growing and ministering together. This was the practice of the desert fathers of the fourth and fifth centuries. We see it in many of the monastic leaders, such as Martin and Benedict, in such Reformation figures as Luther and Melanchthon, Calvin and Bucer (and later Calvin and Beza), in Solomon Stoddard and his grandson Jonathan Edwards, and in John and Charles Wesley.

Over the years I have been involved in many such relationships. Some have been more successful than others. Some lasted only a short time, while others continue to this day. Those that have endured the longest are not necessarily the ones that have involved the greatest investment of time. Indeed, some of my most valuable soul friends live hundreds of miles from me, and I may only speak to them by phone once a month or see them once a year. Still, the help, encouragement, insight, accountability and love they provide are of great benefit to me as I seek to work out my salvation in love to God and others.

Finding a soul friend or two can thus play an important part in helping to get your spiritual disciplines back on track. But how do we go about doing that?

### Finding a Soul Friend

As you seek a soul friend to help in renewing your spiritual disciplines and strengthening your walk with the Lord, you should have a good idea of the kind of person who can best fill this role for you. I have listed the main attributes of a soul friend that I have found to be most helpful. Look for someone—or a few individuals—who embody as many as possible of these traits. Not everyone will have them all, but one or two may. And remember, as the *anamcara* relationship is one of mutual benefit, you must be prepared to be the same kind of person toward whomever agrees to join with you as a soul friend. You may not embody all these attributes at this time. Be honest with your prospective soul friend if that is the case but promise that you will work to become more like what you are looking for in him or her. The relationship itself will help to provide a new focus for your spiritual disciplines as you pray, study, meditate and commune with the Lord concerning how you might become more the *anamcara* that he wants you to be.

So what are the principal attributes required in a soul friend?

*Someone who will pray with you.* First, look for someone who will pray with you both in your times together as well as when you are apart from one another. You want a soul friend who is serious about prayer and will regularly take your burdens as his or her own, bringing them before the throne of grace with the same passion, the same urgency this person would his or her own concerns. The prayers of your soul friend targeted, for example, on the recovery of spiritual disciplines in your life can be crucial to your success in this effort.

Thus, you will want to find someone you know is faithful in prayer, who understands the power of prayer and who practices prayer with a faithfulness that you long to see in your own life. One of my *anamcara*, Brian Bankard, is such a man. I know that he is diligent in prayer for I have been with him both in groups and in private times of prayer, and I have heard the sincerity and passion in his voice. I have seen him carrying around the same lists of prayers for years, dutifully keeping track of requests and answers, and ever seeking new items to bring before the Lord. Brian calls from his home in Kent Island, Maryland, at least once a month, or I call him, and we exchange prayer requests, brief reports on what we have been learning from our time in the Word, and personal words of encouragement, affirmation and love. I cherish his friendship precisely because I know him to be a man faithful in prayer, and his faithfulness helps me to take my own prayers—for him and for others— just that much more seriously. He is both a soul friend and a true friend, and I praise the Lord for bringing us together in this relationship.

*Someone who will give you time.* You and your soul friends will need time together. In some cases this may mean a regular commitment, say, once a week or month. In that time you will renew and expand your friendship, encourage one another in your walk with the Lord, share prayer requests and pray for one another. This will be a time for confrontation as well for your soul friends to challenge you when your disciplines slip or when you are not carrying out the commitments you have made or having trouble reaching the goals you set.

Others and I have found soul friends to be particularly helpful in keeping our witness for Christ alive and active. By sharing with one another the people for whom we are praying, whom the Lord has brought into our lives and are in need of the Savior, soul friends are encouraged to keep working at the process of evangelism in order to reach their neighbors for Christ. Phil Hardin, at the time a pastor in Baltimore, and I were part of a group of five soul friends who met every other week to study evangelism and encourage one another in our witness. A faithful and gifted preacher, Phil admitted that he had let his work in evangelism slide in recent years. Phil committed his witness to the Lord, making growth in this area a central focus of his own spiritual disciplines. Our group was able to encourage him, to pray with him for the people in his neighborhood and community with whom he had regular contact and whom he had determined were in his personal mission field and needed to know the Lord. How we rejoiced with Phil as he gradually got to know his neighbors, engaging them in conversation about spiritual matters and sharing the good news of Christ with them. We grew together during that brief time as each of us made our witness for Christ a more consistent focus of our spiritual disciplines and daily ministry. What a joy it was to be part of Phil's growth in the Lord as a soul friend and to be encouraged by his example and words each time we were together.

But it may not be feasible to spend regular time with your soul friend. Distance, conflicting schedules or other obstacles may get in the way. Yet some time is necessary, even if it is only occasionally on the phone or by e-mail. I am always encouraged to talk with Paul Carter, a pastor in Lexington, Virginia, and a soul friend of many years. His confidence in the Lord, spiritual sensitivity, and winsome and compassionate manner have helped me to keep looking to the Lord for guidance in his Word and strength in prayer through some very difficult times. Paul and I talk occasionally but not with the kind of regularity I might like. Nevertheless, the time he gives me in our conversations and prayers together is more valuable than much of the time I have spent with men in more concentrated, face-to-face situations.

Some time is necessary for soul friends to minister adequately to one another. And each person needs to take some initiative in making sure that time is faithfully kept. Look for someone who understands the importance of this commitment of time and is willing to give some of this precious gift to you.

*Someone you feel free to share with.* It will do no good to enter into a soul friend relationship if you are not willing to be honest about your struggles. Find someone who has an understanding and compassionate heart, will listen to your concerns without judging you and support you in prayer as you work at renewing your spiritual disciplines and growing in grace.

I had met John Armstrong, president of Reformation and Revival Ministries in Wheaton, Illinois, on two occasions: once when he was speaking at a breakfast and again when we were participants together in a discussion in Washington, D.C. We exchanged pleasantries, but that was all. I had read John's books and essays and was impressed with his spiritual insight and sincerity, but we had never spent more than a few minutes together. So I was surprised when, at a time of deep personal confusion and uncertainty, John called me out of the blue to tell me that I had been on his heart and in his prayers. Immediately I felt a kinship that I hoped had come from the Lord. As we talked during that phone conversation, I felt free to share more of the details of my situation with John. He wept, and then he committed to pray for me every day and to check in from time to time to see how we were doing.

He kept his word. Over the ensuing months John called at least once a month. During those times I shared how the Lord had been leading in our lives, how we had been able to discern his will and were now moving into a new and exciting phase of life and ministry. Subsequently John shared with me about his own needs, how he was suffering physically and gravely concerned about his ability to carry on the work to which the Lord had called him. Over the following months my own prayers were strengthened by my commitment to pray for John each day. Knowing that John was praying for me, that he was willing to share with me from his own struggles and concerns, and that we were committed to specific prayers for and accountability with one another provided a much-needed boost for my discipline of prayer at a very critical time in my life.

Since then John and I have been able to spend more time together and have become colleagues in one another's ministries. I feel free to share with John because of his compassionate heart and his own willingness to share with me. Together we have grown because of the relationship that God has given us with one another. He is a true soul friend, and there is at least one like him out there to help you as you work at renewing the disciplines of grace in your life.

Philip Sheldrake explains that in the Celtic tradition, the *anamcara*, according to its original meaning, was one who shared the same cell with another, referring to the monks' habitual dwelling.[6] He was close, close enough to know you as you really are and to care for you at all times. Find someone you would be willing to share your cell with, and you will have found a true soul friend.

*Someone from whom you can learn.* A soul friend should be someone from whom you can learn. Brendan had Bishop Erc to teach him how to pray and open up the treasures of God's Word to him. The bishop remained an *anamcara* for Brendan throughout his life. But The Navigator also had a godly lady, a much older woman, to whom he turned from time to time, Abbess Ita.

Abbess Ita ran a school for boys. Brendan was entrusted to her tutelage for five years, beginning when he was a little over a year old. In her presence he learned the love of God as she surrounded him with tenderness and care. The anonymous author of the late-medieval Irish *Life of Brendan* relates the joy that Brendan knew in Ita's school: "Brendan was always smiling at the nun whenever he saw her. So one day Ita asked him: 'What is it that pleases thee, O holy child?' said she. He answered, 'Thou.'" Immediately after this the writer shows us that this love Ita showed Brendan translated in him into love for others. When Brendan was sent to study with Bishop Erc, "Brig, daughter of Findlug, his [Brendan's] sister, was with him there, and great was his love for her."[7] The only reason for the insertion of this vignette at this point seems to be to show that Ita's influence had taken in the young saint's life. Still later, after his first voyage resulted in failure, and after consulting with Bishop Erc, Brendan went to see Ita to ask her godly advice concerning what to do next. Her advice helped him to succeed in his next mission.

In my own life a godly older woman played a key role as a soul friend. Her name was Pat Hunter, and she was a soul friend to my wife, Susie, as well, and to Susie's parents, Lane and Annette Adams. Susie and I would often go see Pat together, drinking in her joy in the Lord and lapping up her insights into his Word but also cringing under her stern, wagging finger from time to time. From Pat we learned the meaning of trusting the Lord, of taking him at his Word, praying honestly and earnestly before his throne of grace, and obeying his will explicitly. She was a mainstay of grace and truth in our lives for many years.

While a soul-friend relationship is not like mentoring in that the benefits are more mutual, still, your soul friend must be someone from whom you can learn, someone whose insights into the Word of God will spur you on in your own studies and meditations, someone whose prayers and practice of the other disciplines of grace will be a model for you as well. And your soul friend should feel the same way about you.

*Someone who will hold you accountable.* There's an old management adage that says "People do not do what you *ex*pect; they do what you *in*spect." A true soul friend will not hesitate to hold you accountable for commitments that you make together, especially as these concern your use of the disciplines of grace. Look for someone who is not reluctant to take you out to the woodshed from time to time, like Rick Duwe, whom I mentioned in an earlier chapter.

In a soul friend relationship we make commitments to one another, commitments to pray and share from our study of God's Word, our witness to Christ, and our personal needs and concerns. For those commitments to become reality in our lives, we need the grace of God working through his Spirit and through our soul friends. As David Denny has observed:

> Obedience means, in its most radical sense, listening for and following the promptings of the Holy Spirit, which can be mediated by experienced friends who help us along the way. When we are weak, a soul-friend will help hold us to our deepest commitment and highest aspiration.[8]

God is pleased to use others to help us make sure that we carry out the commitments we have made before him. When Jesus sent his disciples out to preach the Word to the villages of Palestine, they knew that he would require an accounting of them, and he did (Lk 10:1-17). One day we shall all give an accounting to the Lord, not only of the use we have made of the disciplines of grace but of our entire life in him as well. Soul friends can help us prepare to hear "Well done, good and faithful servant" by disciplining us for accountability here and now.

*Someone who will stand by you.* No one besides my wife has stood by me quite like my in-laws, Lane and Annette Adams. They have not only been encouragers and affirmers over the past thirty years, but they have also showed the confidence they have in the Lord's calling in my life by opening doors of ministry for me, referring me to other church leaders, to editors and publishers, and to friends in ministry, and by giving me opportunities to serve with them.

The first time Lane did this for me was when he was an associate evangelist with Billy Graham. He was having a crusade in Pekin, Illinois, and since I was a native Illinoisan (and his future son-in-law), he invited me to come and give a personal testimony.

The problem was that I had never given a personal testimony. I had only been a Christian for a couple of years, and not only was this man going to give his daughter's hand to me in marriage, now he was willing for me to come and possibly ruin a whole evening of his crusade. Which I nearly did. I spoke too long, rambled like an untrained preacher, told a couple of not-so-funny jokes, tossed in some irrelevant illustrations and never did quite get around to giving a testimony of the grace of God in my life. But Lane sat there on the platform the whole time, smiling encouragement at me. Afterwards he thanked me—though I had a sickening sense that I had not done what I was supposed to do—and then invited me to join him again in Charleston, West Virginia. This time, he said, I would not only give a testimony (I gathered I was to learn how to do that before then), but I would also be available afterwards to meet with the young people and answer questions about the faith. What a challenge this was to me at this early stage in my walk with the Lord! And how it provided a focus for my growth over the next several weeks. (I'm happy to report that the experience in Charleston was not nearly so disastrous as that in Pekin.)

At difficult times in our marriage and my ministry, Lane and Annette have never failed to be supportive, even when some of my decisions have been, well, not exactly in sync with the Lord's plan or my actions have been less than holy. They have always been honest and forthright with me but loving and supportive at the same time. Find an *anamcara* like Lane and Annette, who will stand with you at all times, and you will find that not only will your use of spiritual disciplines grow stronger, but your walk with the Lord will flourish in new and exciting ways as you grow in love for him and others.

*Where to look.* To be brief, look for someone who embodies as many of these attributes as possible. Don't be afraid to approach a leader in your church or ministry. They may be looking for someone just like you to link up with for a period of time. You may have a friend whose familiarity with you has never probed the spiritual level. Ask him or her to consider entering into this role with you. Maybe there is someone in another church whose ministry you admire but whom you may not know. Get together with that person, share your desire and see what the Lord might do.

If you are married, one place to establish an *anamcara* relationship might be with your spouse. My wife, Susie, is the only soul friend I have ever had who has consistently embodied all of the attributes this role requires. I cherish her prayers, insights and advice more than all my other soul friends put together. The spiritual tie between us has strengthened us both through difficult times, infected us with the joy of the Lord and kept us consistent in our use of spiritual disciplines over the years. Surely this is what God intended for a marriage, two becoming one in flesh and spirit, as they walk together before the Lord in the power of his grace.

As you are beginning to move from routine to renewal in the practice of spiritual disciplines, a soul friend can be a source of great strength and encouragement. Don't try to do this on your own. Seek the Lord's leading in prayer. Let him guide you to someone who understands what you're trying to do, who is seeking renewal himself or herself, and join together before the Lord to "stimulate one another to love and good works." You'll find that this *anamcara* relationship will serve not only to strengthen your use of the disciplines of grace but your walk and ministry in the Lord as well.

### Questions for Review and Discussions

1. Think of some of the soul friends of Scripture—David and Jonathan, Daniel and his friends, Barnabas and Paul. How can you see

that each member in this relationship benefited from what the Lord was doing in the life of the other(s)?

2. What fears do you have about beginning such a relationship? Are they reasonable? How might you use the disciplines of grace to begin dealing with these fears?

3. Can you think of anyone who might be a good candidate to be an *anamcara* with you? Why does this person come to mind? What might you have to offer him or her?

4. This relationship will require time. Your schedule may have to change somewhat. As you think about beginning a soul friend relationship, what will you be willing to give up in order to have the time this will require?

5. What would you like to see happen in your use of the disciplines of grace as a result of entering into a soul friend relationship? How might doing so help you to realize the goals you have established for this study?

# 11

# DISCIPLINING YOUR ROUTINES

*The only true source of discipline in this world is fellowship with Christ.*
*The moment Jesus Christ really comes into a person's life, he finds a new*
*discipline, one which is no longer rigid, formalist, or heavy, but joyous, supple,*
*and spontaneous. Discipline is not the goal of life, nor even a means of coming to*
*Christ. It is a consequence of the change in outlook which takes place*
*when Christ breaks into a person's life.*
PAUL TOURNIER

*If ye then be risen with Christ, seek those things which are above,*
*where Christ sitteth on the right hand of God.*
*Set your affection on things above, not on things on the earth.*
COLOSSIANS 3:1-2

*F*or the better part of thirteen years my drive to work was a half-hour either way. For the first few of those years it was a tedious, monotonous routine. I would get in the car, turn on the radio and half-listen to the news or classical music as I fought the traffic on the Baltimore beltway. Sometimes my mind would drift ahead to the work that was before me, only to be distracted before much serious thought could take hold by someone cutting me off or some slowdown in traffic, either of which would make my blood pressure rise and summon up the beast of anger from the pit of my soul.

At other times I would occupy myself by reading license plates. With our children we used to play a game of making words out of the letters on license plates. Whoever made the shortest word first, following the order of letters on the license plate, won the point. I won a lot of points those first several years as I drove to work.

Ultimately a more frivolous diversion took over. I started counting the number of plastic bags that I would see waving in the breeze in the trees and bushes along the road. Some stayed in place for a long time, joined each day by new roadside immigrants from who knows where. I would even report my daily total to Susie when I got home in the evening, as though I were taking some significant census each day.

I also enjoyed reading bumper stickers and vanity license plates, and would try my hand at making up a sticker or tag of my own, one that I might be willing to display. (My favorite vanity plate, seen on Route 66 in northern Virginia, was on a Swedish import. It read "SNAAB.")

All these diversions helped the time go a little faster during the inevitable and necessary routine of getting to work and home again each day. They didn't require much effort or thought, and they kept me from getting too irritated at other drivers (I often wondered what they were doing to keep from becoming irritated with me). These diversions were part of my routine, helping me to maintain my patience and sanity in what I came to regard as a necessary evil, driving to and from the office.

In retrospect I realize that they were a huge waste of time, for I have come to see that even the routines of our lives can be taken captive for the purposes of growth in Christ and for helping us to keep seeking the things that are above, where Christ is seated in the heavenly places. We can find joyous, supple and spontaneous fellowship with the Lord Jesus even in the midst of the most tiresome, tedious and mindless routines. All we need to do is learn how to bring a little discipline to each one of them.

Routines, as we saw in chapter one, are both inevitable and necessary. They may not cost us much in terms of time or mental energy, but they help us maintain a certain status quo that is important to our well-being. Each of us adheres to a wide range of routines—at home, at the office, in our personal lives and elsewhere. We don't give much thought to them; rather, we just go through them—routinely, as it were—getting on to the more important matters in life once we have accomplished these mindless activities that help us bridge to bigger things. We can't avoid our routines, so we might as well learn how to make the most of them for our walk with the Lord.

**Grace in the Ordinary**

Susie and I had never had a vacation of our own. The children had always been along no matter where we went, and it was difficult for us to enjoy much in the way of meaningful time alone together. So when our children finally reached the age that the youngest ones of them could care for themselves, we decided to take a week off together and make a tour of some of the local Civil War battlefields. We started at Gettysburg, drove south to Antietam, then headed to Manassas before ending up in Williamsburg for a weekend of colonial Americana. Ever the Civil War buff, I decided to bone up on my knowledge of the places and players we would be encountering along the way in our journey.

I was reading R. L. Dabney's *Life and Campaigns of Lieut.-Gen. Thomas J. Jackson*. Stonewall Jackson played major roles in the battles of Bull Run (Manassas) and Antietam, and he was mortally wounded by friendly fire at the Battle of Chancellorsville. As Jackson lay dying, the true spiritual nature of the man came out in ways that struck me like the clapper of a cathedral bell:

> During these morning hours, he delighted to enlarge on his favorite topics of practical religion; which were such as these: The Christian should carry his religion into everything. Christianity makes man better in any lawful calling; it equally makes the general a better commander, and the shoemaker a better mechanic. In the case of the cobbler, or the tailor, for instance, religion will produce more care in promising work, more punctuality, and more fidelity in executing it, from conscientious motives; and these homely examples were fair illustrations of its value in more exalted functions. So, prayer aids any man, in any lawful business, not only by bringing down the divine blessing, which is its direct and primary object, but by harmonizing his own mind and heart. In the commander of an army at the critical hour, it calmed his perplexities, moderated his anxieties, steadied the scales of judgment, and thus preserved him from exaggerated and rash conclusions. Again he urged, that every act of man's life should be a religious act. He recited with much pleasure, the ideas of Doddridge, where he pictured himself as spiritualizing every act of his daily life; as thinking when he washed himself, of the cleansing blood of Calvary; as praying while he put on his garments, that he might be clothed with the righteousness of the saints; as endeavoring, while he was eating, to feed on the Bread of Heaven.[1]

It was as if the Lord himself were speaking to me about the routines of my own life. I did not have to invent frivolous, mindless ways of getting through these routines each day; instead, I could discipline them for the purposes of God's kingdom, bringing even my routines into the joy of encountering the Lord and growing in his grace. Thus began an exciting new phase in my own spiritual growth and in the use of the disciplines of grace in my life. I started to discipline my routines, taking them captive and making them obedient to the purposes of the Lord Jesus Christ in my life, learning to employ even the most mundane moments of my daily life for the cause of our heavenly King.

In this chapter I share some of the ways disciplining my routines brings a more spiritual outlook into the whole of my life and strengthens my use of the disciplines of grace but keeps them from becoming mere routines themselves.[2] I have found, as Paul Tournier indicates in the quote above, that once my outlook on my routines changed as a result of my desire to be in fellowship with Christ as much as possible, discipline could become a way of life, helping me to keep growing closer to the Lord, even at the most unlikely of times. I have begun to understand something of what Jonathan Edwards meant when he wrote:

> So we ought to subordinate all our other business, and all our temporal enjoyments, to this affair of travelling (*sic*) to heaven. Thus we should eat and drink and clothe ourselves and improve our conversation and enjoyment of friends. And whatever business we are setting about, whatever design we are engaging in, we should inquire with ourselves, whether this business or undertaking will forward us in our way to heaven![3]

The suggestions that follow may be of help to you in bringing the grace of spiritual disciplines into the routines of your everyday life, thus allowing you to engage even mundane moments in growing in love for God and others.

### Disciplining Your Daily Preparations

I used to begrudge my time of getting ready for the day. How often I longed for the luxury of so many college students who simply roll out of bed in the morning, splash some water in their faces, throw on whatever clothes are lying around and head off for class. I remember once, during a chapel service at a Christian college, seeing some of the women in attendance in their pajamas, their hair still in hot curlers for the day ahead, the men looking as if they had been carried in on their beds. How much easier and more enjoyable my life would be, I used to think, if I didn't have to spend that thirty minutes every morning shaving, showering, fussing with my hair and trying to decide what to wear.

That was before Stonewall Jackson. After I read the passage cited above, I began to consider my morning routine with a different outlook, seeing in that half-hour an opportunity for spending time with the Lord in a more complete preparation for the day. I began to experiment with various activities. First, instead of classical music on the radio, I started listening to world and national news, with an ear for things I might pray about as I was getting ready. I remember once in particular, when floods were ravaging the eastern seaboard of the United States, hearing the report of the devastation on National Public Radio and praying earnestly that God would mobilize his churches to reach out and care for the people whose homes and businesses were under water. What a delight it was, while I was still praying, to hear included in that same report a segment on how churches were beginning to do precisely that. On another occasion I recall hearing the testimony of a Christian woman who had undertaken some good work in her community out of her sense of commitment to Christ, and I was able to praise the Lord both for her testimony and the fair and positive way NPR presented the report. Many such opportunities for intercession and prayer have presented themselves as I get ready for the day.

I started disciplining specific routines within my morning routine — shaving, showering and dressing, for example. As I lather up and drag my razor across my face, I pray that the Lord will shape and mold me during the day ahead, working on my mind, heart and life to make me the person he wants me to be. I try to recall my devotions from the previous day, asking the Lord to work in my life according to what he showed me then. Particular projects, meetings, people, activities or responsibilities will frequently come to mind, and I will be reminded to ask the Lord to shape and use me in those opportunities for his glory. My shower is a time for seeking the cleansing of my soul as well as my body. I pray for the Lord to reveal any unknown sin in me and to cleanse me heart, mind and life from any filth of transgression that may yet be clinging to me. Following my shower I like to put on a little after-shave, and this is a time for asking the Lord to make me a fragrance of Jesus to everyone I will meet that day (2 Cor 2:15-16). I often pray briefly for specific people or meetings, that I may show the love of Christ while I am with them. As I dress, I pray to be clothed with the righteousness of Christ and the good deeds of the saints (Rev 19:8), even to the point of seeking specific aspects of the fruit of the Spirit for situations I expect to encounter during the day or that I am reminded of from recent devotions. Then I head down to the kitchen to make coffee, by which time my heart is overflowing with praise and thanks to God for this wondrous roasted bean and the brilliant, creative and anonymous genius who discovered its God-appointed purpose.

Sound a little corny? Perhaps a little contrived? I can understand that you might think so. But be assured that I do not find these activities corny or contrived. Nor do I find them rigid, formalist or heavy. Indeed, I would not think of starting my day, of going through the routines of getting cleaned up, dressed and ready to go, without seeking the fellowship of the Lord in the midst of them. These morning routines have become such a time of sheer enjoyment of the Lord and eager anticipation of the day ahead that I cannot imagine going back to the mindless, begrudging execution of them that characterized my morning preparations for all those years. By disciplining these routines I have known more of the presence of the Lord, have sensed his glory accompanying me even in trivial activities as these, and find my heart and mind better prepared for the rest of the day.

### Disciplining Your Meals

Here I must confess that I write as an eager aspirant. In my home as I was growing up, when you sat down to eat, you ate. You did not engage in conversation, whether frivolous or profound, because, if you did, one of those other hungry hulks sitting at the table would snarf up the last piece of meat loaf. We ate with a purpose, which was to get as much food as we could until we were full. When we were finished, we left the table, whether everyone else was done or not.

I am trying to be more subject to the disciplines of grace during this time, especially during the meals I take at home. First, I try to ensure that my prayer before dinner is not merely perfunctory. I will take my time, thinking of any pressing issues so that I can bring them before the Lord (safety for a traveling child, help with a critical decision, or the needs of those who have less than we do, for example). I will thank the Lord for all his goodness, of which this meal is but a token, often naming specific items. During the meal I am trying to be a more conversational person, trying to engage our time together for mutual growth and encouragement (progress is slow; pray for me). Edwards remarks on the value of godly conversation to enhance our growth in the Lord. Following his advice, I am trying to "be more disposed to enter on such conversation as would be for [our] mutual edification and instruction"[4] by engaging Susie about her morning devotions, sharing what the Lord is showing me or seeking his will with her concerning some matter. I have also found that if I take a hand in, say, setting the table or cleaning up the kitchen, it gives me an opportunity for thanking the Lord for his goodness to us, even in the details of dinnerware and kitchen facilities—things I don't usually think of during my normal times of prayer.

Throughout the meal, moreover, I try to keep in mind Jackson's observation of Doddridge about feeding on Christ. I love to savor the rich variety of flavors and textures that Susie puts before me each night, and I often think, as I am doing so, about the infinite goodness of Jesus, his many wonderful traits and gifts, and the sheer enjoyment of knowing him. As I comment to Susie on how much I am enjoying the meal, I thank the Lord for her and for the abundance with which he has blessed us. I have a real sense of the Lord's presence with us at the table, and I am filled with rejoicing in him as much as with the cuisine.

### Disciplining Your Drive Time

Which of us would not like to know a little more of the presence of the Lord during drive time? We are not, after all, immune to the temptation of road rage. Surely the peace that passes understanding and the joy of the Lord would be much more welcome affections as we inch and weave our way along in traffic?

Three disciplines in particular have been helpful to me while driving. The first is meditation. While I have my radio on or a cassette tape in the deck, I'm thinking about the beauty and goodness of the Lord as I hear it in the music, observe it in the creation around me or contemplate it in the evidences of human culture on every hand. None of these things exists apart from the goodness of God. He has given them to us in order to make himself known, that we might contemplate him, delight in his gifts and benefits, and seek and love him more and more. As I pay careful attention to these things, the words of Scripture from one or another place will come to mind, enhancing and enriching my meditation and leading me to prayer and praise. Often, as I have thanked the Lord for highway workers and prayed for their safety, I have been led to thank and praise him for the work that he has entrusted to me. What sweet joy I have known to see a family of deer browsing on a hillside or when a wild turkey soared over the top of my car and landed in a field on the other side of the road.

As I observe all these things and think about the majesty, greatness, goodness and power of the Lord, I feel great joy in his love for me and in his ability to keep me in his care and provide for all my needs. My faith rises to new heights of confidence and satisfaction. Driving in the car provides many prompts and stimuli that we normally take for granted, our minds busied during this routine activity with many distractions and anxious concerns. But drive time can be, as we work to discipline this routine, an opportunity for drawing us into seasons of meditation and rich fellowship with the Lord Jesus Christ.

Drive time has also provided many opportunities for prayer. Indeed, prayer is a discipline that can fill up any of the routines of our lives, as Clement of Alexandria observed when he said that the sincere Christian will pray "in every place . . . but not ostensibly and visibly to the multitude. . . . But while engaged in walking, in conversation, while in silence, while engaged in reading and in works according to reason, he in every mood prays."[5]

In two ways especially I have had some success in using prayer to discipline this daily routine. The first way is using prayer cards, a discipline I learned from Archie Parrish. From time to time it has been my practice as part of my morning devotions to write the names and addresses of people on my prayer list on a postcard, together with a message to the effect, "I have prayed for you today and want you to know that I love you in the Lord." Then I put a stamp on the postcard and put it in my briefcase or diary. As I drive along, I pull those cards out—maybe four or five of them—and offer prayer for the people whose names I wrote on the cards earlier. Then, when I reach my destination, I simply drop them in the mail. The apostle Paul seemed to think there was some benefit to be gained on the part of those for whom we pray if we not only pray for them but let them know that we are (Eph 1:15; Col 1:9). On many occasions those for whom I have prayed have called to thank me, both for the prayer and for the note. And not infrequently, as it turns out, those prayers were offered at a very important time in the person's life. But my time in prayer for them was just as important to me in helping me to discipline the routine of getting to work.

The second way prayer helps me in disciplining the routine of drive time is by my looking and listening for prompts to prayer. At times, as I have previously mentioned, a person comes into my mind. We have all experienced this on occasion. Normally we let the thought of these people pass out of our consciousness on its way to who knows where. But Paul seemed to take such fleeting thoughts as prompts to prayer from the Spirit of God, as he told the Philippians in Philippians 1:3: "I thank my God in all my remembrance of you." So when people come to mind as I drive, I offer a prayer of thanks to the Lord for them, using that time to ponder all the ways that God has blessed me through such people or to think about some particular need on their part of which I may be aware. Then I seek his blessing for them in prayer, that the remainder of the day may be unto his glory and for their profit.

Other things serve as prompts to prayer as well: a broken-down car on the side of the road or an accident will lead me to intercede for the Lord's help for the people involved and ask that they might know that he is their help so that they may join the ranks of those who daily praise and thank him. Beautiful vistas along the way—of which there is no shortage here in West Virginia—bring forth prayers of praise and thanks to God. News reports, beautiful music, even the wonders of the internal combustion engine that keeps me safely and smoothly gliding along will draw out prayers of intercession or of gratitude and rejoicing in the goodness of the Lord.

The key is to learn to "persevere in prayer" (Rom 12:12 NRSV), to be ready and able to turn to prayer and enter into the fellowship of the Lord so as to make the most of the opportunities for encountering him and growing in his grace that our daily routines routinely provide. We are commanded in Scripture to "pray without ceasing" (1 Thess 5:17 NRSV), and while we never achieve that ideal in this life, surely there are ways that we can recover something that so many of us do so much of—time driving in the car[6]—for this wonderful privilege and rich discipline of grace.

The third discipline I have found helpful in taking this routine captive for growth in Christ is that of singing, which is another form of prayer. What better place for making a joyful noise unto the Lord than in the solitude of your own vehicle, with only the Lord for your audience? I will sing along with a cassette of Gregorian chant or work my way through some favorite hymns or praise songs. Time flies by and my heart is lifted as I think about the lyrics and immerse myself in the melodies, not just singing in my heart but belting it out as loudly as I please in the joy and rejoicing of the Lord.

I'll make a little confession here. (I suppose it's a confession because I'm not prepared to recommend this practice for everyone.) I was driving home from work one evening when I was passed on the right by an older gentleman who was huffing away on a harmonica, a sheet of music spread out before him on the steering wheel. I was intrigued, to say the least. Then, about a week later, I heard essayist Bailey White on NPR tell of her experience of playing the harmonica while driving and how it lifted her spirits and made the drive across Georgia seem much shorter. So I went out and bought a harmonica, began to learn to play it a little, and now find great joy in whining out everything from Gregorian and Gaelic chants to traditional hymns to praise songs, Irish laments and even an original tune or two while I am driving along in my car. As I said, I don't recommend this practice for everyone (although I'm convinced it's safer than talking on a cell phone). But I have found it a wonderful way of enjoying the fellowship of the Lord in song while I am driving, particularly when I am on a long trip.

The time we spend in our cars does not have to be wasted in anxious fretting, mindless musings or otherwise wasted moments. It can be captured and disciplined for the cause of knowing the Lord, entering into his glory and delighting in him in wonderful and exciting ways.

### Disciplining Your Work Routines

Abba Lucius, a fourth-century ascetic, once chided a group of monks who were disparaging manual labor because they found it to be a distraction from their heavenly callings. He told them they should learn to discipline the routines of their work in order to fulfill their callings from the Lord:

I will show you how, while doing my manual work, I pray without interruption. I sit down with God, soaking my reeds and plaiting my ropes, and I say, "God, have mercy on me, according to your great goodness and according to the multitude of your mercies, save me from my sins . . ." So when I have spent the whole day working and praying, making thirteen pieces of money more or less, I put two pieces of money outside the door and I pay for my food with the rest of the money . . . so, by the grace of God, I fulfill the precept to pray without ceasing.[7]

Abba Lucius had learned the secret of disciplining the routines of his daily work for the purposes of Christian growth.

Much of what I have said applies, with appropriate modifications, to the disciplining of our work routines—meetings, phone calls, paperwork, the details of assembling, packaging, processing, exchanging, shipping, selling, buying, planning, reporting, reviewing and everything else that makes up the daily grind of our work. The same can be said for the work we do at home. There is time for meeting with the Lord in our housecleaning, yard work, routine maintenance and repairs, marketing, and all the errands and chores that it takes to keep a household running and thriving.

Much of what we begrudge about our work is related to the tedium and boredom that we experience in these various tasks. They can sometimes seem like necessary evils or unwelcome intrusions into our otherwise exciting life. We're forever looking for some way to make our work more interesting and efficient or for someone else to do it for us. Alternately, we procrastinate on certain matters for as long as we can, just because we resent having to take the time to submit to the routines that this work requires. Frankly, much of what we have to do to keep food on the table and a roof over our heads just isn't that much fun.

So let's remember—not only for our work, but all our routines as well—what G. Campbell Morgan taught about the way that the disciplines of grace can bring new meaning, purpose and power into all of life, including our work: "In *the interaction of life and prayer* will be found the secret of power, and the realization of fellowship with God will never be more than a theory save as prayer becomes a practice."[8] The "interaction of life and prayer." He might just as well have added meditation and singing to the Lord to that as well. What Morgan calls for is nothing less than the purpose of this chapter, namely, to help you to find ways of creating more intersections with the divine presence, more fellowship with God, in the interstices of life where we submit to various routines in order to keep our lives moving on and moving ahead. This is what learning to discipline our routines is all about, so that, as Clement of Alexandria wrote, our whole life becomes a time of "holding festival" with God. That will be our experience when, "persuaded that God is altogether on every side present, we cultivate our fields, praising; we sail the sea, hymning; in all the rest of our conversation we conduct ourselves according to rule,"[9] that is, discipline.

In disciplining the routines of my own work I have found a few simple practices to be of enormous help. The first is to take seriously the apostolic injunction: "Be anxious for nothing, but *in everything* by prayer and supplication with thanksgiving let your requests be made known to God" (Phil 4:6, emphasis added). Every routine of work is an opportunity for turning to the Lord in prayer, be it ever so brief. It is a summons to refocus our thoughts on things above, where Christ is seated in the heavenly places, and to enter into all our work activities as unto the Lord, not men (Col 3:23). Rather than begrudge or avoid that stack of phone calls to be returned, that lawn to be mowed, those dirty dishes and clothes, that weekly sales meeting, all those studies or all that paperwork, we must learn to see these as opportunities for thanking the Lord for the work he has given us to do and for seeking his blessing in making that work as productive and enjoyable as it can be. For years I have followed the practice of committing my work to the Lord each day, and as often as I remember to do so during the day, by praying the prayer of Moses in Psalm 90:16-17, which I paraphrase thus: "Lord, show me the work you have for me today, and make your glory known to me in the midst of it. Bless me as I undertake the work you have given me to do; confirm my work, and affirm me in it, Lord; and let me do all that I do for your glory." This simple prayer, which hangs on a poster in my study, has remarkable effects in helping to keep my work in a proper perspective and to keep me mindful of the Lord's presence in all my work (Ps 139:7-12).

In this same vein I have found it helpful to set aside some time during the workday to stop what I am doing, tearing myself away from my business (to paraphrase Tertullian)[10] to devote some time to the Lord. Usually at midmorning and midafternoon, as well as at lunch, I will draw aside to be with the Lord for a few moments of meditation and prayer, guided by one or more of the psalms. While it is relatively easy for me to do this now that I work at home, I observed this discipline even when I served as a seminary president. I would tell my assistant that I would be unavailable for a few moments and ask her to hold my calls. Or I would just draw back at my desk and retire into my spirit for this precious time of fellowship with the Lord. Even if you can't actually draw aside to a different place, taking five minutes at your desk or station is not impossible. If Daniel, who administered an entire empire, could find the time for this discipline (Dan 6:10), surely we can carve it out as well and use these times of drawing aside for prayer as ways to discipline the routines of work that await us when we return.

Second, I have made it a point over the years to pay careful attention, during my devotions and other times in the Word, to Scriptures that seem to speak directly to my particular work, whatever it may be. I have tried to memorize those verses and, as I was doing so, meditate on their meaning for my own work. And I have found that doing so has helped to bring new light on and new delight to my work routines. For example, I have hated lawn work ever since I was a kid. It took so much time and involved mindless pushing, trimming and edging that drained my energy and wasted an otherwise perfectly good day. Several years ago, however, I was working on a series of lessons on the subject of a biblical view of work. I searched the Scriptures for relevant texts and spent a great deal of time studying and thinking about the meaning of those passages for me. One passage that I recall having a profound impact was Genesis 2:8-15. I meditated on the beauty of the garden and the great responsibility entrusted to Adam, to work on that beauty so that it might become even more fruitful and bountiful. How he must have delighted to take up this work each day with a view to magnifying the goodness of God with his own hands.

That passage had a profound effect on me relative to my responsibility for caring for our yard. I began to see our yard as our own little part of God's garden, and my responsibility to care for it as a calling to bring out the goodness of God in what he had entrusted to me. While I'm no landscape expert, I have come to enjoy cutting my grass and trimming the yard, working in our garden and everything that goes with these activities. As I am mowing the grass, edging the yard or hoeing the garden, I find myself praising God for this part of his creation that he has allowed me to care for. I ask him to bless my efforts to make it beautiful and good, to give me strength to serve him in this work and to give pleasure to my family, neighbors and visitors as a result of my work. I will often find myself singing in the midst of my yard work or marveling at the various bugs and wildflowers that crop up in our lawn. I thank God for the machinery and tools that he has provided for me in this work, the sweat that pours from my brow, and even the sore muscles with which I am sometimes blessed. I have come to enjoy and even look forward to my time working in the yard, for it is no longer a tedious, tiresome routine but a season of fellowship with the living God in which, through meditation and prayer, I experience his presence with me and delight in the work he has given me to do.

Work does not have to be something that we resent or merely force ourselves to do. By disciplining the routines of work we can know the presence of God in the interstices of our work life and be buoyed up by his Spirit and Word as we bask in the wonder of his transforming glory and grace. As with all the suggestions I have made in this chapter, learning to do this will take some time and concentrated effort—we are talking about disciplines, after all, not mindless routines. But the benefits of devoting ourselves to disciplining our routines can be so many and wonderful, that we shall marvel that we did not take the time to do this sooner.

### The Benefits of Disciplining Our Routines

Numerous benefits of disciplining our routines await those who undertake this challenge. I have already suggested several of these in my comments above, so I can perhaps summarize them in what follows. I will mention five benefits that I have found from devoting myself to disciplining my routines day in and day out.

*Capturing dead time for spiritual renewal.* First, giving ourselves to the task of disciplining our routines enables us to capture what we may regard as *dead time* for truly lively purposes. Instead of mindlessly plodding through our routines each day, gaining only the maintenance benefit they afford, we may seize and transform them as opportunities for growing in grace. We will not, of course, regard such times as our primary involvement in the disciplines of grace, but like the condiments that enhance our meals, disciplining our routines can help to salt our daily lives with the presence of God, bringing us more consistently into the orbit of his Word and Spirit and exposing us to his life-changing glory in ways we might otherwise never realize. Time that we may previously have begrudged or avoided can be captured for most lively and significant encounters with the living God.

*Actualizing the presence of God.* Second, disciplining our routines serves to make real and vital to us the fact of God's constant presence with us throughout the day. While it is easy amid the distractions and routines of daily life to lose sight of the Lord and feel as though we have drifted away from him, the fact remains that he is with us always, that no matter where we go or what we are doing, we can never escape the loving, caring presence of his Spirit (Ps 139:7-12; Mt 28:20). How wonderful it is to be able to realize that constant care more consistently, to know the presence and fellowship of the Lord in even the most mundane and routine activities of life.

*Benefiting others.* Third, the suggestions we have examined above can only serve to benefit those for whom we pray and intercede as we discipline the routines of our daily lives. Prayer is powerful and can move the hands of God in wondrous ways to meet the needs of those we love and care about. It only stands to reason that the more of such prayer we can add to our day, the greater the likelihood that our prayers will result in blessing to those who are the objects of our intercessions and pleadings before the throne of grace.

*Seeking the Lord in all things.* Fourth, disciplining our routines helps to train our minds and hearts to keep seeking the Lord in all things. I have found it to be more and more true that in every situation of my life — whether triumph or trial, difficulty or deliverance — my mind turns immediately to the Lord in thanksgiving and supplication (Phil 4:6-7). This has not always been the case. For long years in my life, trial or difficulty would lead to feeling sorry for myself, worry or even anger and resentment. Victories and deliverances would issue in a sense of relief and a clinging to whatever material circumstance, person or thing was the secondary cause in the divine scheme for my well-being. In recent years, however, my spiritual screensaver has learned to default to the Lord Jesus Christ, enthroned in all his glory at the right hand of the Father, putting his enemies under his feet, subduing all things for the purpose of building up his people and working all things together for good in my life (Rom 8:28; 1 Cor 15:25-28; Eph 1:20-23; Col 3:1-2). I can tell you that a life of thanks, praise and expectant trust is much to be preferred to one of anxiousness and dread, or delight in merely temporal circumstances and things.

*Strengthening the disciplines of grace.* Fifth, disciplining our routines strengthens our use of the disciplines of grace at other times as well, thus providing one more means of helping us to turn our spiritual routines into spiritual disciplines once again. A little salt can go a long way in improving a person's consumption. By exercising our spiritual muscles in the routines of life, we strengthen them for more effective use in those times we have set aside to enter these special arenas of grace that the spiritual disciplines provide. We learn to sense the glory of God more effectively and to draw on the power of his Word and Spirit with greater benefit. Our mind is trained to become more attentive. Our heart grows more sensitive. Our desire for a transformed life becomes evermore fervent. Our love for God and for our neighbors is more constantly engaged and thus more likely to grow stronger as, having learned to discipline our daily routines, we enter into those special arenas of grace that are the spiritual disciplines of the Lord.

Of course, your concern is that these activities can become trivial or merely formal. And, of course, they can and probably will at times. But this does not mean they necessarily have to or that, just because they sometimes do, they have no benefit. Disciplining our routines is not the goal of life or of the practice of spiritual disciplines. But once we see our daily routines as opportunities for spending more time with our Lord, for entering more constantly and effectively into the fellowship of his Word and Spirit, to behold his glory and know his transforming power in our lives, we will want to capture as much of this time as possible to make it available for the practice of spiritual disciplines and serve the purpose of Christian growth in our lives. And, as we do this, we will find these times to be the joyous, supple and spontaneous encounters with the Lord that can help in the process of making all things new in our lives.

## Questions for Study or Discussion

  1. Be honest: What is your immediate response to this chapter? Why?
  2. Can you see ways that you might discipline the routines of your

life? Explain.

3. How might you expect to benefit from trying this? How would you expect this to affect your practice of spiritual disciplines at other times?

4. What can keep you from disciplining your routines? How can you overcome those obstacles?

5. What have you learned from this chapter? How has it challenged you? How do you think this might help you to reach the goals you set for this study?

# 12

# RUNNING the RaCe
# WITH patience

*B*efore we conclude our study of the disciplines of grace, we need to establish a final point about spiritual exercises and spiritual growth, lest any misconceptions find their way into our practice of spiritual disciplines. Two are possible. I have mentioned these before, but they deserve a somewhat fuller exposure.

The first is that practicing the disciplines of grace can always be expected to yield an experience of high spiritual exhilaration. While it is true that, in these special arenas of grace, we navigate the deep waters of spiritual life in the glorious presence of God's Word and Spirit, it is not true that we always experience the disciplines in just that way. In fact, much of our time spent in the practice of spiritual disciplines can seem fairly routine and uneventful.

While I urge you to seek a higher plane of involvement with the Lord in the practice of spiritual disciplines, I would not want you to feel like a failure should you discover that your experience is often something less. The point is to press on, seek the higher ground and cry out to the Lord to show you his glory and transform you more and more into the image of Christ. There is great power available and tremendous excitement in the practice of spiritual disciplines. The same is true in playing the piano. But in each case, until we master the basics and devote ourselves with real staying power and intensity to the task, we are not going to know much of that power or excitement. And even once we have begun to know this kind of experience, our continuing sinfulness will surely make it difficult, if not impossible, for us to sustain it without interruption.

The challenge is to keep the objective in view—what God promises in terms of showing us his glory, and how we can expect to grow in love for him and others—and to "run the race" of the disciplines with unflagging resolve, making such adjustments as are needed from time to time in order to realize that objective more and more.

The second, and perhaps more important, misconception relates to the results of spiritual discipline and the process of growth. As Luder Whitlock points out so well in his book *The Spiritual Quest*, spiritual growth is like physical growth in many ways. Change is gradual and can often only be identified in retrospect. We will not spring from our practice of the disciplines of grace into full-blown Christian maturity. Rather, as we gain new and more exciting glimpses of the Lord, we will discover, often after the fact, ways that we have grown in love for him—heart, mind and strength—and for our neighbors as ourselves. We will see that we have begun to trust in him, call on him and obey him more willingly and completely in the daily grind of discipleship and that, as a result, we are not the people we used to be, still chained to the same old sins or locked into the same tiresome patterns of self-centered disobedience. Rather, we will be able to see areas where our attitudes have changed, our understanding has grown, and our lives have taken on a greater degree of faithfulness as we have persevered in the disciplines of grace.

Such changes come gradually for the most part. Thus, once again our calling is to press on, run the race and stay the course in the belief that God, who alone can give spiritual growth, will do so in his own ways and time.

I want to bring our study of the disciplines of grace to a conclusion by recommending something of a metastructure for the long haul, an overarching pattern for growing in grace that, together with the practice of spiritual disciplines, can help us keep our eyes on Jesus and run our race with real perseverance and power.

### Disciplining the Walk

The purpose of spiritual disciplines is to help us grow in the Lord, to bring our walk—heart, mind and life—more and more into agreement with the heart and mind of God and his purposes for our lives. When our disciplines lapse into mere routines, they cannot serve this purpose. At best they can merely keep us on some kind of spiritual plateau; however, not a very high one and not for very long. If we are not growing—not loving the Lord and our neighbors as we should—we need to look at our practice of the disciplines of grace. For it may well be that we need to reassess our practice, either increasing or intensifying it, adding new disciplines, finding a soul friend, working to discipline our daily routines, or focusing our time in the disciplines of grace more precisely and carefully. From the disciplines of grace comes spiritual strength for growth and transformation. Any attempt to change our ways without shoring up the spiritual foundations of our lives will ultimately come to naught.

Yet we must always remember that the disciplines of grace are not ends in themselves. They are means to the end of loving God and our neighbors, of growing into an unhypocritical walk with Lord. We always need to guard against the temptation of thinking that the mere practice of spiritual disciplines is all that God requires of us. He is at work within us to will and do of his good pleasure (Phil 2:12-13), and his good pleasure is that we should love him and our neighbors more and more. Sometimes our encounters with him in the disciplines of grace will be full and rich; at other times they will be more subdued and uneventful. Yet, consistently practiced and improved, the disciplines of grace can be expected to yield a life of progressive growth in the Lord and fruitfulness for his glory. For this to result from our practice of the disciplines of grace will require three further disciplines, each of which is generated from within the disciplines of grace and leads us out from them into glorious transformation in Christ.

*The discipline of repentance.* The first is the discipline of repentance. I should rather say the *grace* of repentance, for while repentance is something that we must practice, it is first of all a gift of God. Unless he gives us repentance from ungodly ways, we shall in no way be able to realize it in our lives.

Repentance is a complete change of mind, so strong and forceful that it brings the heart and life into line along with it, leading to changes of attitude and behavior. In repentance we come to see things in a new light—God's light:

> By it, a sinner, out of the sight and sense not only of the danger but also of the filthiness and odiousness of his sins, as contrary to the holy nature, and righteous law of God; and upon the apprehension of his mercy in Christ to such as are penitent, so grieves for and hates his sins, as to turn from them all unto God, purposing and endeavouring to walk with him in all the ways of his commandments.[1]

Repentance radically affects our attitude toward sin. The sin that we have newly discovered or been comfortable with for so long suddenly becomes so despicable that we cannot wait to be done with it. We see it as the holy God does. We understand that it was for such sin that Christ went to the cross, and we come to despise the sin, resolving to rid ourselves of it by every means at our disposal.

Yet everything in our sinful lives resists the call to repentance. Nothing in our mortal strength is sufficient to engender it. Thus, we must ever seek repentance from the Lord, for if we are to have it, he must give it. Using the disciplines of grace to discover and lead us to confess our sinful ways, and as a context within which to plead with the Father of light for the gift of repentance, we may come to attain it in his power and time. Whether the repentance we require is for some newly discovered or lingering sin, or for some failure in the practice of spiritual disciplines, we may be assured that God will grant it as we persist in seeking it from him by faith.

Here Paul's statement that we "walk by faith, not by sight" (2 Cor 5:7) is particularly apt. The idea of walking refers to our conduct of every aspect of daily life—preparing for the day, taking meals, going through the routines of work and home, taking diversion and everything else that makes up our days, including the practice of spiritual disciplines. The conduct of all these activities must be "by faith," for "whatsoever *is* not of faith is sin" (Rom 14:23). That is, in all these activities our minds and hearts must be set on the Lord—to see his glory and love him more—so that our lives will follow in the course he desires for us—that of loving our neighbors as ourselves. We must be ever alert to the fact that our adversary, the devil, constantly seeks to distract our minds and hearts from Christ, to draw our affections away to worldly enticements and to suggest ways of rationalizing disobedience to our weak and sinful minds (1 Pet 5:8; 1 Jn 4:1-6). As we strengthen our use of spiritual disciplines, our minds will grow stronger in the Lord, our hearts will become more pure, and we will find in us a greater readiness to seek the gift of repentance from the Lord whenever we come to recognize that such is our need. We will see our need of repentance more readily, long for it more devotedly and seize it more wholeheartedly as we grow in love for God and our neighbor, and as he grants us the grace of repentance. Repentance is absolutely crucial to the disciplining of our daily walk. Without it we shall never realize any lasting progress in faith.

Therefore, let us seek the Lord for repentance in all our ways, beginning with the practice of spiritual disciplines and leading out from there into every aspect of our lives in Christ.

*The discipline of faith and obedience.* But we must go on from repentance to faith and obedience in the Lord. If we merely sweep the house clean of wickedness without establishing new practices in its place, we can be sure that wickedness will be back again in abundance (Mt 12:43-45). Repentance turns us away from that which is displeasing to God; faith and obedience take us on into the newness of life in Christ. Disciplined minds and hearts will be eager for such newness. They will have understood, envisioned and embraced it. But only as we go forward in confidence in the Lord will we realize the promise of transformation that comes from repentance and faith, and that results in loving God and others more. As Jesus said (Jn 13:17), if we know these things—know them so that we love them, so that our minds are fully committed to them and our hearts completely enthralled with them—and if, through the grace of repentance and faithful obedience, we do them, we will be blessed with the transforming power of God to make all things new in our lives.

Obedience typically comes in small steps. We are prompted to take some seemingly trivial initiative—to speak a word of kindness, extend a gesture of love, share a word of testimony, confess a transgression against another—which to us hardly seems the stuff of martyrs. But fidelity in the small things leads to readiness to obey in the large.

We should expect, in our practice of spiritual disciplines, that very often people and their needs will come to our minds, as well as things we might do to address those needs. As we commune with the Lord and he ministers to us by his Word and Spirit, we may fully expect him to give us such insights and make his counsel known. We will demonstrate faith and obedience when we act with diligence on these promptings. As we spread the practice of spiritual disciplines into new areas and throughout our day, we can expect such promptings to increase. Our faith will grow and our obedience be made more complete as we follow each of these promptings as a mission from the Lord, repenting of our disdain for small things and believing instead that these are the tokens of love that God requires of us for now and that may lead to greater opportunities for service in the days to come. "He that is faithful in that which is least is faithful also in much" (Lk 16:10).

But once again, even the faith to obey the Lord and to act on the things he has impressed on us must come from him. Thus, along with repentance, we must cry out for the Lord to enable us to act on the weak faith we have and to increase that faith so that we may obey him more readily and fully.

*The discipline of thanksgiving.* A final discipline that must arch over every area of our lives, from our practice of spiritual disciplines to the whole of our walk with the Lord, is the discipline of thanksgiving. An argument could be made that thanklessness is the greatest sin of our generation. Read the catalog of ills presented by the apostle Paul in Romans 1:24-32: uncleanness, lust, sexual perversity, deceitfulness, violence, strife, lack of mercy and all the rest. What is the cause of this moral degradation that has become so commonplace in our day? It is the failure to give thanks (vv. 18-21) and turning from faith in the living God to faith in devices and schemes of one's own choosing (vv. 22-23). Thanklessness leads to idolatry; idolatry leads to sin; sin brings the judgment of God against a people and its culture.

The place to heal this wound is in the lives of those who know the Lord and who would live disciplined, repentant and obedient lives before him. We must recover the discipline of thanksgiving as a declaration of unflinching faith in God and the key to peace in the face of every difficulty or trial.

Recall how often and with what passion and sweeping comprehensiveness the apostle Paul called the followers of Christ to thanksgiving: "Be careful for nothing; but in every thing by prayer and supplication with thanksgiving let your requests be made known unto God" (Phil 4:6); "That ye might walk worthy of the Lord unto all pleasing . . . giving thanks unto the Father" (Col 1:10, 12); "In every thing give thanks: for this is the will of God in Christ Jesus concerning you" (1 Thess 5:18). Clearly Paul intended the readers of his words to cultivate the discipline of thanksgiving, come what may.

By giving thanks always in all things we show our confidence in God's sovereign rule, express our belief that he is working all things together for good, and act in faith to wait on him for that good outworking in our lives. By failing to give thanks we evidence a lack of faith in all these areas, walk by sight and stumble into sin. Our spiritual disciplines may be weak, even nonexistent. We can thank the Lord for showing us this and cry out for the grace of repentance and the gift of faith and obedience. We may have entered a dark night of the soul. Let us give thanks, recall the goodness of the Lord and show our intention of waiting on him in thanksgiving until that goodness is renewed (Ps 13). We may be rejoicing in his favor, suffering under his discipline, perplexed, exhilarated, confused, convinced, resolved or unclear. In all these and more, let us learn to give thanks.

Note also that we are to give thanks *in* all things but not necessarily *for* all things. There is a subtle difference. We may properly show indignation at sin perpetrated against us, express sorrow for suffering (ours or others') and be impatient with and pray for the removal of hindrances to growth. We need not give thanks *for* such things. Yet we must give thanks *in* them, showing God our confidence in him and in his goodness, and expressing our determination to trust in him and look to him until he brings his goodness to light in our lives. Giving thanks *in* all things reminds us that God himself is our ultimate good, he knows what is best for us at all times, and he will never fail us nor forsake us (Ps 16:2; 73:28; Heb 13:5). We will not despair in seeking the goodness of God through thanksgiving, for we know that he is faithful and just and will not allow us to be tested beyond what we are capable of bearing but will, with the test, provide a way of escape in his way and time (Ps 27:13-14; 1 Cor 10:13).

Nor will we wait to give thanks until we *feel* thankful, for that is to walk by sight and not by faith. We will thank the Lord *in* faith, looking to him to change our affections as need be and trusting in him to do what is good in our lives.

These three disciplines—repentance, faith and obedience, and thanksgiving—can only be nurtured in the practice of spiritual disciplines. In that rich soil they grow and take root in our lives, where they further strengthen the practice of spiritual disciplines and help us grow in love for God and others.

## Despise Not Disciplines

The practice of spiritual disciplines is hard work, and for a comfort-saturated generation such as ours, renewing those disciplines will be even harder. But let it not be said of us, as it was of those wicked Israelites who worshiped among the people of God in Asaph's day, that we despise the disciplines of the Lord (Ps 50:16-17). Instead let us labor to recover the right practice of the disciplines of grace, reclaiming them from being mere routines until they become the engines of grace and renewal that God intends them to be. Then we will discover again what it means to walk in the fullness of life, glorifying and enjoying God, loving him and our neighbors with the grace that turns the world upside down for Christ. At the same time let us cultivate repentance, faith and obedience, and thanksgiving from within as well as beyond the practice of spiritual disciplines as an overarching framework of discipline for our lives in Christ. Surely thus we may hope to move from routine to renewal and to know the transforming grace and power of Christ more fully in our lives.

## Questions for Study or Discussion

1. Have you begun to determine any areas in your practice of the disciplines of grace where you might have need of repentance? Explain.

2. How can you see that repentance, faith and obedience, and thanksgiving must be kept in place as overarching disciplines in the life of faith? Can we expect our practice of the disciplines of grace to produce any lasting change apart from these? Why not?

3. How has your approach to the practice of spiritual disciplines been affected by this study? What changes have you made or do you need to make?

4. In what specific ways would you like to see renewal in the practice of spiritual disciplines affect your love for God? For your neighbor?

5. As you see it, what is the single most important lesson you take away from these studies? How will you apply that lesson to your life?

# Notes

### Chapter 1: Disciplines or Routines?

[1] Dallas Willard, *The Divine Conspiracy* (New York: HarperCollins, 1998), p. 353.

[2] For biblical examples of the glory of God expressing his presence, see Exodus 24:16-17; 40:34-35; 2 Chronicles 7:1-3; Isaiah 6:1-5.

[3] Jonathan Edwards, "A Divine and Supernatural Light," in *The Works of Jonathan Edwards*, ed. Edward Hickman (Edinburgh, Scotland: Banner of Truth Trust, 1995), 2:13.

[4] Ibid., 2:17.

[5] See some of the books mentioned in the following chapters.

[6] Eliza E. Hewitt, "More About Jesus Would I Know," in *Trinity Hymnal*, rev. ed. (Atlanta: Great Commission, 1990), p. 538.

### Chapter 2: The Powers of God & the Disciplines of Grace

[1] See, for example, the holy sonnets of John Donne; Mark A. Noll, *Seasons of Grace* (Grand Rapids, Mich.: Baker, 1998); John Leax, *Out Walking* (Grand Rapids, Mich.: Baker, 2000).

[2] Jonathan Edwards, "The Distinguishing Marks of a Work of the Spirit of God," in *The Works of Jonathan Edwards*, ed. Edward Hickman (Edinburgh, Scotland: Banner of Truth Trust, 1995), 2:268.

[3] Luder G. Whitlock Jr., *The Spiritual Quest* (Grand Rapids, Mich.: Baker, 2000), pp. 28-29.

[4] Martin Luther, "The Pagan Servitude of the Church," in *Martin Luther: Selections from His Writings*, ed. John Dillenberger (New York: Doubleday, 1961), pp. 274-82.

[5] Roman Catholic theologian David Denny acknowledges the principle of *ex opere operato* but writes that "this must be balanced by the approach . . . which stresses that we must prepare ourselves carefully, mindfully, and prayerfully for spiritual disciplines." David Denny, "The Circle and the Cross," *The Chesterton Review* 26, no. 1 and 2 (2000): 156.

[6] Luther, "Pagan Servitude," p. 275.

[7] Matthew Henry's admonition is apt here: "We shall see how little reason we have to be proud of our knowledge when we consider how many things we are ignorant of." *Matthew Henry Commentaries: Acts* (New York: Revell, n.d.), 6:6.

[8] Helmut Thielicke, *A Little Exercise for Young Theologians* (Grand Rapids, Mich.: Eerdmans, 1994), p. 12.

[9] See Luther's "The Freedom of the Christian," in *Martin Luther: Selections from His Writings*, ed. John Dillenberger (New York: Doubleday, 1961), p. 67.

### Chapter 3: The Disciplines of Grace

[1] Besides Dallas Willard's *The Spirit of the Disciplines* (New York: HarperCollins, 1991), I have found the following books to be helpful in nurturing the spiritual life: Dietrich Bonhoeffer, *Life Together*, trans. John W. Doberstein (San Francisco: HarperSanFrancisco, 1954); Richard J. Foster and James Bryan Smith, *Devotional Classics* (San Francisco: HarperSanFrancisco, 1989); Mark Harris, *Companions for Your Spiritual Journey* (Downers

Grove, Ill.: InterVarsity Press, 1999); Evan B. Howard, *Praying the Scriptures* (Downers Grove, Ill.: InterVarsity Press, 1999); Bill Hybels, *Too Busy Not to Pray* (Downers Grove, Ill.: InterVarsity Press, 1998); Abraham Kuyper, *The Practice of Godliness*, trans. and ed. Marian M. Schoolland (Grand Rapids, Mich.: Baker, 1948); Kathleen Norris, *The Cloister Walk* (New York: Riverhead, 1996); Eugene H. Peterson, *Answering God* (San Francisco: HarperSanFrancisco, 1989); Douglas D. Webster, *Soulcraft* (Downers Grove, Ill.: Inter-Varsity Press, 1999); Luder G. Whitlock Jr., *The Spiritual Quest* (Grand Rapids, Mich.: Baker, 2000); Dallas Willard, *Hearing God* (Downers Grove, Ill.: InterVarsity Press, 1999). Readers may wish to consult some of the classic literature on the spiritual life as well. An excellent bibliography can be found in the acknowledgments section of Foster and Smith.

[2]Furthermore, I am here only dealing with those disciplines that might be described as "active disciplines," or those we enter into freely of our own accord. There are also passive disciplines that the Lord brings to us according to his sovereign mercy—the disciplines of trial, temptation, chastening and conviction, for example—but I shall have nothing to say concerning these at this point. I hope to write a book on growing through these passive disciplines at some point in the future.

[3]For a sample of these devotional guides call Scripture Union at 1-800-621-LAMP.

[4]For an excellent guide in how to undertake such study of God's Word, see Gordon D. Fee and Douglas Stuart, *How to Read the Bible for All Its Worth* (Grand Rapids, Mich.: Zondervan, 1993).

[5]Benedicta Ward, *The Sayings of the Desert Fathers* (Kalamazoo, Mich.: Cistercian, 1984), p. 22.

[6]C. S. Lewis, *The Screwtape Letters* (New York: Simon & Schuster, 1961), p. 28.

[7]See also Bruce B. Barton, gen. ed., *The One Year Book of Bible Prayers* (Wheaton, Ill.: Tyndale House, 2000), and Ken Boa, *Handbook to Prayer* (Atlanta: Trinity House, 1993).

[8]For fuller discussions of the purpose and elements of worship, as well as contemporary issues in worship, see John M. Frame, *Worship in Spirit and Truth* (Philipsburg, N.J.: Presbyterian & Reformed, 1996); Donald P. Hustad, *True Worship* (Wheaton, Ill.: Harold Shaw, 1998); Sally Morgenthaler, *Worship Evangelism* (Grand Rapids, Mich.: Zondervan, 1995); Robert G. Rayburn, *O Come, Let Us Worship* (Grand Rapids, Mich.: Baker, 1987); Bard Thompson, ed., *Liturgies of the Western Church* (Philadelphia: Fortress, 1980); Robert E. Webber, *Worship Old and New* (Grand Rapids, Mich.: Zondervan, 1982).

### Chapter 4: The Goal of Spiritual Disciplines

[1]Benedicta Ward, *The Sayings of the Desert Fathers* (Kalamazoo, Mich.: Cistercian, 1984), p. 8.

[2]Jonathan Edwards, "The Christian Pilgrim," in *The Works of Jonathan Edwards*, ed. Edward Hickman (Edinburgh, Scotland: Banner of Truth Trust, 1995), 2:244.

[3]Augustine, *Soliloquies*, in *Nicene and Post-Nicene Fathers*, ed. Philip Schaff (Peabody, Mass.: Hendrickson, 1995), 1:541-42.

[4]Dallas Willard, *The Divine Conspiracy* (New York: HarperCollins, 1998), p. 324 (my emphasis).

[5]Let us not be confused or misled about the idea of *ministry*. In the minds of some readers ministry may conjure up such tasks as feeding the poor, preaching the gospel or going to the mission field. And while it is true that these are among the works of ministry God approves, yet many more humble, simple and readily available works fall into this category as well. Dietrich Bonhoeffer, in his book *Life Together*, provides a wonderful catalogue of such works, including everything from the ministry of holding one's tongue or

being a good listener to those of helping and evangelizing ([New York: HarperCollins, 1954], pp. 90-109).

[6]Jonathan Edwards, *The Religious Affections* (Edinburgh, Scotland: Banner of Truth Trust, 1986), p. 29.

[7]Ibid., p. 27.

[8]Cf. Harry Blamires, *The Christian Mind* (Ann Arbor, Mich.: Servant, 1978), and Mark A. Noll, *The Scandal of the Evangelical Mind* (Grand Rapids, Mich.: Eerdmans, 1994).

[9]Jonathan Edwards, "Christian Knowledge," in *The Works of Jonathan Edwards*, ed. Edward Hickman (Edinburgh, Scotland: Banner of Truth Trust, 1995), 2:157.

[10]Ibid., 2:158.

[11]Ibid., 2:162.

[12]To reiterate the seven helpful suggestions that Edwards makes in his sermon on Christian knowledge: (1) be assiduous in reading the Scriptures; (2) don't be content with a merely cursory reading; study to grasp the sense of a passage; (3) read sound Christian literature; (4) talk with others about spiritual things; (5) always have a mind to how what you are learning will affect your life; (6) ask God to direct and bless your studies; and (7) practice what you are learning in your everyday life (ibid., 2:162-63).

[13]Francis A. Schaeffer, *True Spirituality* (Wheaton, Ill.: Tyndale House, 1973), p. 60.

### Chapter 5: Preparing for Renewal in Prayer

[1]Augustine, *The City of God*, 1.3.14, trans. John Healey, ed. R. V. G. Tasker (London: Everyman's Library, 1967), p. 89.

[2]If you added Psalms 19, 25 and 33, you would have twenty-five psalms focusing on the Word and will of God, which you could add to your twenty-five days of praying the questions in chapters one through five.

### Chapter 6: A Question of Priorities

[1]*Westminster Confession of Faith*, 18.9.

[2]Bill Hybels, *Too Busy Not to Pray* (Downers Grove, Ill.: InterVarsity Press, 1998), p. 126.

[3]Jonathan Edwards, "The Preciousness of Time," in *The Works of Jonathan Edwards*, ed. Edward Hickman (Edinburgh, Scotland: Banner of Truth Trust, 1995), 2:233.

[4]Ibid., 2:234.

[5]Ibid., 2:235.

[6]Neil Postman, *Amusing Ourselves to Death* (New York: Penguin, 1985).

[7]Ibid., pp. 114-24.

[8]"It is easier to be physically active in order to be spiritually indolent." Simon Chan, *Spiritual Theology* (Downers Grove, Ill.: InterVarsity Press, 1998), p. 75.

[9]Jonathan Edwards, "Christian Knowledge," in *The Works of Jonathan Edwards*, ed. Edward Hickman (Edinburgh, Scotland: Banner of Truth Trust, 1995), 2:161.

[10]Edwards, "Preciousness of Time," 2:236.

[11]Stephanie Winston, *Everything in Its Place: Conquering Paper Clutter* (Emmaus, Penn.: Rodale, 2000).

### Chapter 7: Redeeming the Time

[1]Jonathan Edwards, "The Preciousness of Time," in *The Works of Jonathan Edwards*, ed. Edward Hickman (Edinburgh, Scotland: Banner of Truth Trust, 1995), 2:236.

[2]Ibid.

[3]Tertullian, "On Prayer," in *Ante-Nicene Fathers*, ed. Alexander Roberts and James Donald-

son (Peabody, Mass.: Hendrickson, 1995), pp. 689-90.

[4]Edwards, "Preciousness of Time," 2:235.

### Chapter 8: Intensifying the Time

[1]Richard Peace, *Spiritual Journaling: Recording Your Journey Toward God* (Colorado Springs: NavPress, 1995), p. 9.

[2]Mark Harris, *Companions for Your Spiritual Journey* (Downers Grove, Ill.: InterVarsity Press, 1999), p. 55.

[3]Ronald Quillo, *The Psalms: Prayers of Many Moods* (Mahwah, N.J.: Paulist, 1998), pp. 11-15.

[4]Eugene H. Peterson, *Answering God: The Psalms as Tools for Prayer* (New York: HarperCollins, 1989), p. 108.

[5]Cf. Daniel's prayer in Daniel 9 (esp. v. 5), Psalm 106:6 and Acts 4:23 (cf. Ps 2:1-2; 146:6).

[6]Published in *Christianity and the Arts* (Spring 2000): 11. Used by permission of the author.

[7]You may be thinking, *John Calvin? He was into singing?* Calvin had a high regard for singing in worship, which he learned from Martin Bucer during his period of exile in Strasbourg. See Bernard Cottret, *Calvin: A Biography* (Grand Rapids, Mich.: Eerdmans, 2000), p. 173. For examples of some of Calvin's own Scripture songs, see Ford Lewis Battles, trans. and ed., and Stanley Tagg, music ed., *The Piety of John Calvin* (Grand Rapids, Mich.: Baker, 1978), p. 137.

[8]John Calvin, foreword to *The Geneva Psalter*, in *Source Readings in Music History: The Renaissance*, ed. Oliver Strunk (New York: W. W. Norton, 1965), p. 158.

[9]*Trinity Psalter* (Pittsburgh: Crown and Covenant Publications, 1994).

[10]Many others have made this same observation concerning Dr. Boice.

[11]I know of no better place to point you for beginning to study worship than volume 9, numbers 2 and 3 of *Reformation and Revival Journal* (Reformation & Revival Ministries, P.O. Box 88216, Carol Stream, IL, 60188-0216).

[12]Some suggestions for beginning to study chant: The little book *Chant: The Origins, Form, Practice, and Healing Power of Gregorian Chant* by Katherine Le Mee (New York: Bell Tower, 1994), is probably the best place to begin. An accompanying cassette tape series from Pharaoh Audiobooks (346 Route 214, P.O. Box 535, Phoenicia, NY 12464, 1-800-688-2535) provides many excellent examples of Le Mee's text. The three-CD series *Eternal Chant* (Atlantic Recording, 1994) includes a brief but helpful introductory booklet and lyrics in the original language and English. For a deeper study (but not as deep as, say, Willi Apel, David Hiley or *The New Oxford History of Music*, vol. 2) see Richard L. Crocker, *An Introduction to Gregorian Chant* (New Haven, Conn.: Yale University Press, 2000). I am listening to the accompanying CD for this volume as I write these words.

### Chapter 9: Innovating Disciplines

[1]*Constitutions of the Holy Apostles*, in *Ante-Nicene Fathers*, ed. Alexander Roberts and James Donaldson (Peabody, Mass.: Hendrickson, 1995), 7:469.

[2]Abraham Kuyper, *The Practice of Godliness* (Grand Rapids, Mich.: Baker, 1977), p. 100.

[3]This is the whole point of Tertullian's tract "On Fasting," in *Ante-Nicene Fathers*, ed. Alexander Roberts and James Donaldson (Peabody, Mass.: Hendrickson, 1995), 4:102-14. Tertullian's concluding comment—obviously with a view of the martyrs—is a challenge to us all: "An overly-fed Christian will be more necessary to bears and lions, perchance, than to God."

[4]Ibid., 4:106.

[5]Ibid., 4:110.

[6]Dallas Willard, *The Spirit of the Disciplines* (New York: HarperCollins, 1991), p. 160.

[7]Personal correspondence, December 2, 2000.

[8]Philip Sheldrake, *Living Between Worlds: Place and Journey in Celtic Spirituality* (Cambridge, Mass.: Cowley, 1995), p. 73.

[9]Kenneth Hurlstone Jackson, ed., "The Hermit's Hut," in *A Celtic Miscellany* (London, England: Penguin, 1971), pp. 68-70.

[10]Sheldrake, *Living Between Worlds*, p. 80.

## Chapter 10: Finding a Soul Friend

[1]For an explanation of the Irish view of penance as remediation, see Thomas O'Loughlin, *Celtic Theology* (London and New York: Continuum, 2000), p. 52.

[2]In Charles Plummer, ed. and trans., *Lives of Irish Saints* (Oxford, England: Oxford University Press, 1997), 2:46.

[3]For an introduction to this little-known period of church history, see Thomas Cahill, *How the Irish Saved Civilization* (New York: Doubleday, 1995), and T. M. Moore, "The Second Wave," *Reformation and Revival Journal* 8, no. 4 (1999): 147.

[4]Esther De Waal, *The Celtic Way of Prayer* (New York: Doubleday, 1997), pp. 134, 137.

[5]For a fuller treatment of this last example, see Robert E. Coleman, *The Master Plan of Evangelism* (Old Tappan, N.J.: Revell, 1987), and Leighton Ford, *Transforming Leadership* (Downers Grove, Ill.: InterVarsity Press, 1991).

[6]Philip Sheldrake, *Living Between Worlds: Place and Journey in Celtic Spirituality* (Cambridge, Mass.: Cowley, 1995), p. 44.

[7]Plummer, *Lives of Irish Saints*, 2:45-46.

[8]David Denny, "The Circle and the Cross," *The Chesterton Review* 26, no. 1 and 2 (2000): 153-54.

## Chapter 11: Disciplining Your Routines

[1]R. L. Dabney, *Life and Campaigns of Lieut.-Gen. Thomas J. Jackson* (Harrisonburg, Va.: Sprinkle, 1983), pp. 713-14.

[2]I beg the reader's indulgence here. I feel like the apostle Paul in 2 Corinthians 11:1: "I wish you would bear with me in a little foolishness. Do bear with me!" (NRSV).

[3]Jonathan Edwards, "The Christian Pilgrim," in *The Works of Jonathan Edwards*, ed. Edward Hickman (Edinburgh, Scotland: Banner of Truth Trust, 1995), 2:244.

[4]Jonathan Edwards, "Christian Knowledge," in *The Works of Jonathan Edwards*, ed. Edward Hickman (Edinburgh, Scotland: Banner of Truth Trust, 1995), 2:162.

[5]Clement of Alexandria, *The Stromata*, in *Ante-Nicene Fathers*, ed. Alexander Roberts and James Donaldson (Peabody, Mass.: Hendrickson, 1995), 2:537.

[6]Some readers may resonate well with a bumper sticker I saw recently: "If I'm a stay-at-home mom, why do I spend so much time in the car?"

[7]Benedicta Ward, *The Sayings of the Desert Fathers* (Kalamazoo, Mich.: Cistercian, 1984), p. 121.

[8]G. Campbell Morgan, *The Practice of Prayer* (Grand Rapids, Mich.: Baker, 1971), p. 13 (emphasis added).

[9]Clement of Alexandria, *Stromata*, p. 533.

[10]Tertullian, "On Prayer," in *Ante-Nicene Fathers*, ed. Alexander Roberts and James Donaldson (Peabody, Mass.: Hendrickson, 1995), 4:690.

## Chapter 12: Running the Race with Patience

[1]*Westminster Confession of Faith*, 15.2.

11008

11008

6/2/02   Rohn
         Jennifer Cleveland
5/29/2013  Linda Simpson